JUNG
CONTRA
FREUD

From

The Collected Works of C. G. Jung
Volume 4, Part 2
Bollingen Series XX

JUNG
CONTRA
FREUD

The 1912 New York Lectures on the
Theory of Psychoanalysis

C. G. Jung

With an introduction by
Sonu Shamdasani

Translated by R.F.C. Hull

PHILEMON SERIES

Published with the support of the Philemon Foundation
This book is part of the Philemon Series of the
Philemon Foundation

BOLLINGEN SERIES

PRINCETON UNIVERSITY PRESS
PRINCETON AND OXFORD

Published by Princeton University Press, 41 William Street,
Princeton, New Jersey 08540
press.princeton.edu

Cover photographs: (left) *Portrait of Carl Gustav Jung*, Switzerland, January 1, 1904.
Courtesy of the Collection of Hulton Archive/Photo by Imagno/Getty Images. (right)
Sigmund Freud, Austria, ca. 1906. Courtesy of the Collection of Archive Photos/Photo
by Imagno/Getty Images.

Extracted from *Freud and Psychoanalysis*, volume 4 of the *Collected Works of C. G. Jung*,
pages 83–226. All the volumes comprising the *Collected Works* constitute number XX in
Bollingen Series, sponsored by Bollingen Foundation.

Library of Congress Control Number: 2011933118
ISBN (cloth): 978-0-691-15418-3
ISBN (pbk.): 978-0-691-15251-6

Printed on acid-free paper. ∞
Printed in the United States of America
10 9 8 7 6 5 4 3 2 1

CONTENTS

INTRODUCTION BY SONU SHAMDASANI   vii

The Theory of Psychoanalysis   1

Foreword to the First Edition   3

Foreword to the Second Edition   5

1. A Review of the Early Hypotheses   6

2. The Theory of Infantile Sexuality   20

3. The Concept of Libido   29

4. Neurosis and Aetiological Factors in Childhood   47

5. The Fantasies of the Unconscious   57

6. The Oedipus Complex   69

7. The Aetiology of Neurosis   75

8. Therapeutic Principles of Psychoanalysis   99

9. A Case of Neurosis in a Child   122

INTRODUCTION: JUNG, NEW YORK, 1912

Sonu Shamdasani

September 28, 1912. The *New York Times* featured a full-page interview with Jung on the problems confronting America, with a portrait photo entitled "America Facing Its Most Tragic Moment"— the first prominent feature of psychoanalysis in the *Times*. It was Jung, the *Times* correctly reported, who "brought Dr. Freud to the recognition of the older school of psychology." The *Times* went on to say, "[H]is classrooms are crowded with students eager to understand what seems to many to be an almost miraculous treatment. His clinics are crowded with medical cases which have baffled other doctors, and he is here in America to lecture on his subject." Jung was the man of the hour. Aged thirty-seven, he had just completed a five-hundred-page magnum opus, *Transformations and Symbols of the Libido,* the second installment of which had just appeared in print. Following his first visit to America in 1909, it was he, and not Freud, who had been invited back by Smith Ely Jelliffe to lecture on psychoanalysis in the new international extension course in medicine at Fordham University, where he would also be awarded his second honorary degree (others invited included the psychiatrist William Alanson White and the neurologist Henry Head).

Jung's initial title for his lectures was "Mental Mechanisms in Health and Disease." By the time he got to composing them, the title had become simply "The Theory of Psychoanalysis." Jung commenced his introduction to the lectures by indicating that he intended to outline his attitude to Freud's guiding principles, noting that a reader would likely react with astonishment that it had taken him ten years to do so. The explanation lay in the fact that when he first encountered Freud's work, he did not feel in a position to exercise criticism. To understand this more fully, we need to look back at Jung's initial engagement with psychoanalysis.

ENGAGING WITH FREUD

After his medical studies, Jung took up a post as an assistant physician at Burghölzli hospital at the end of 1900. The Burghölzli was a progressive university clinic under the directorship of Eugen Bleuler. Thanks to Bleuler and his predecessor, Auguste Forel, psychological research and hypnosis played prominent roles at the Burghölzli. One of Jung's first assignments was to present a report on Freud's recently published short digest of *The Interpretation of Dreams, On Dreams*. In his report, Jung concluded that Freud's approach to dreams was somewhat one-sided, as the cause of a dream could equally be an undisguised repressed fear, as well as a wish.[1]

In 1902, Jung left his post at the Burghölzli and went to Paris to study with the leading French psychologist Pierre Janet, who was lecturing at the Collège de France. After his return, he took up a recently vacated post at the Burghölzli and devoted his research to the analysis of linguistic associations, in collaboration with Franz Riklin. With coworkers, they conducted an extensive series of experiments. Jung and Riklin utilized the association experiment, devised by Francis Galton and developed in psychology and psychiatry by Wilhelm Wundt, Emil Kraepelin, and Gustav Aschaffenburg. The aim of the research project, instigated by Bleuler, was to provide a quick and reliable means for differential diagnosis. The Burghölzli team failed to come up with this, but they were struck by the significance of disturbances of reaction and prolonged response times. Jung and Riklin argued that these disturbed reactions were due to the presence of emotionally stressed complexes, and they used their experiments to develop a general psychology of complexes.[2]

This work established Jung's reputation as one of the rising stars of psychiatry. The conceptual basis of his early work lay in the work of Théodore Flournoy and Janet, which he attempted to fuse with the research methodology of Wilhelm Wundt and Emil Kraepelin. In such a manner, he was attempting to develop a clinico-experi-

---

[1] C. G. Jung, "Sigmund Freud: *On Dreams* (1901)," in *The Collected Works of C. G. Jung* (hereafter *CW*), ed. Sir Herbert Read, Michael Fordham, and Gerhard Adler; William McGuire, Executive Editor; tr. R.F.C. Hull; Bollingen Series XX (Princeton, N.J.: Princeton University Press, 1953–1983), vol. 18, § 869.

[2] "Experimental Researches on the Associations of the Healthy (1904)," *CW* 2.

mental method, which he termed experimental psychopathology. The appearance this gave of being able to conduct psychotherapy in a scientific manner, through adopting some of the procedures of the experimental laboratory, did much to ensure the popularity of Jung's associations research, particularly in America.[3] The leading psychiatrist Adolf Meyer hailed Jung and Riklin's first paper in laudatory terms: "This remarkable piece of work and its continuation are no doubt the best single contribution to psychopathology during the past year."[4]

In 1904, Bleuler introduced psychoanalysis into the Burghölzli, and entered into a correspondence with Freud.[5] Jung noted the proximity of his work on the association experiment to Freud's concept of repression.[6] In 1906, Jung expanded on this connection in a paper on "Psychoanalysis and the Association Experiment." He noted that while psychoanalysis remained a difficult art, the association experiment offered a secure framework for finding essential data, which removed haphazardness in therapy.[7]

Jung's proposition astutely caught the mood of the psychiatric world, and his version of the association experiment spread like wildfire, particularly in America. A steady stream of American visitors, including George Amden, Abraham Brill, Trigant Burrow, August Hoch, Charles Ricksher, Frederick Peterson, and E. W. Scripture, came to work with Bleuler and Jung at the Burghölzli,

[3] See Eugene Taylor, "Jung before Freud, not Freud before Jung: The Reception of Jung's Work in American Psychotherapeutic Circles between 1904 and 1909," *Journal of Analytical Psychology* 43, 1998, pp. 97–114.
[4] *Psychological Bulletin*, 1905, p. 242. On Meyer and Jung, see Ruth Leys, "Meyer, Jung and the Limits of Association," *Bulletin of the History of Medicine* 59, 1985, pp. 345–60.
[5] Freud archives, Library of Congress. See Ernst Falzeder, "The Story of an Ambivalent Relationship: Sigmund Freud and Eugen Bleuler," *Journal of Analytical Psychology* 52, 2007, pp. 343–68.
[6] See C. G. Jung, *Introduction to Jungian Psychology: Notes of the Seminar on Analytical Psychology Given in 1925*, revised edition, ed. Sonu Shamdasani, original ed. William McGuire (Princeton, N.J.: Princeton University Press, 2012), p. 14.
[7] *CW* 2, § 663. In retrospect, Jung stressed the significant differences between Freud's concept of repression and his dissociative model—Richard Evans (1957), "Interview with C. G. Jung," in William McGuire and R.F.C. Hull, eds., *C. G. Jung Speaking: Interviews and Encounters*, Bollingen Series (Princeton, N.J.: Princeton University Press, 1977), p. 283. On this question, see John Haule, "From Somnambulism to Archetypes: The French Roots of Jung's Split from Freud," *Psychoanalytic Review* 71, 1984, pp. 95–107; and my "From Geneva to Zurich: Jung and French Switzerland," *Journal of Analytical Psychology* 43, 1, 1998, pp. 115–26.

and to study their psychological approach to psychopathology. For American psychiatrists, the interest in the psychogenesis of symptomatology seemed a notable advance over the descriptive and classificatory approach of Kraepelin. In 1907, after studying with Kraepelin in Munich, Frederick Peterson went to Zurich, and wrote his impressions to Adolf Meyer: "I have met Von Monakow here and of course see a great deal of Bleuler and Jung. I am delighted with everything in Zürich and am sorry that I spent so long a time at Munich. Jung is in every way charming and I think he has genius."[8] Together with his coworkers, Jung published a series of articles in American journals.[9]

In 1906, Jung entered into communication with Freud. This relationship has been much mythologized. A Freudocentric legend arose, which viewed Freud and psychoanalysis as the principal source for Jung's work. This has led to the complete mislocation of his work in the intellectual history of the twentieth century. On numerous occasions, Jung protested. For instance, in an unpublished article written in the 1930s, "The Schism in the Freudian School," he wrote: "I in no way exclusively stem from Freud. I had my scientific attitude and the theory of complexes before I met Freud. The teachers that influenced me above all are Bleuler, Pierre Janet, and Theodore Flournoy."[10] Freud and Jung clearly came from quite different intellectual traditions, and were drawn together by shared interests in the psychogenesis of mental disorders and psychotherapy. Their intention was to form a scientific psychotherapy based on the new psychology and, in turn, to ground psychology on the in-depth clinical investigation of individual lives. Jung described his initial attitude toward Freud in a letter he wrote to his colleague Dumeng Bezzola shortly after meeting Freud for the first time in 1907:

[8] Frederick Peterson to Adolf Meyer, 21 January 1907, Adolf Meyer Papers, Johns Hopkins archive.
[9] C. G. Jung, "On the Psychophysical Relations of the Associative Experiment," *Journal of Abnormal Psychology* 1, 1907, pp. 247–55; with Frederick Peterson, "Psycho-Physical Investigations with the Galvanometer and Pneumograph in Normal and Insane Individuals," *Brain* 30, 1908, pp. 153–218; with Charles Ricksher, "Further Investigations on the Galvanic Phenomenon and Respiration in Normal and Insane Individuals," *Journal of Abnormal Psychology* 2, 1908, pp. 189–217.
[10] Jung papers, Swiss Federal Institute of Technology, Zurich.

We can still not correct [Freud], since we still know far too little; I have experienced this to my deepest shame. . . . I have therefore decided no longer to correct or to oppose Freud; I simply leave what I still do not understand to one side, and perhaps mark it with a question mark.[11]

From 1906 until 1913, a series of debates about psychoanalysis took place in psychiatric congresses. It is striking that despite invitations, Freud himself did not take part. Instead, it was Jung who took up the task of publicly defending psychoanalysis in open debate. Jung later recalled to Kurt Eissler, "[Freud] never risked himself in a congress and never defended his cause in public! . . . This always made him afraid! America was the first and only time! . . . He was too touchy!"[12] Within the German psychiatric community, Freud, as a neurologist in private practice, did not have a strong reputation. However, when his views were defended by respectable psychiatrists such as Bleuler and Jung, they had to be taken seriously. In reply to Gustav Aschaffenburg in 1906, Jung argued that the only way to disprove this was to use Freud's method: "As soon as Aschaffenburg meets these requirements, that is to say, publishes psychanalyses with totally different results, we will have faith in his criticism, and then the discussion of Freud's theory can be opened."[13] This became one of the key rejoinders to Freud's critics.

In 1907, Jung applied his new theory of complexes to study the psychogenesis of dementia praecox (later called schizophrenia), and to demonstrate the intelligibility of delusional formations.[14] In his preface, he noted,

Even a superficial glance at the pages of my work will show how much I have to thank the ingenious conceptions of Freud. . . . I can affirm that in the beginning I naturally made all the objections that are customarily made against Freud in the literature. But I said to myself, Freud could be refuted

[11] Jung to Bezzola, 23 April 1907, Bezzola papers, courtesy of Angela Graf-Nold.
[12] Transcription of Eissler's interview with Jung, 29 August 1953 (original in German); Sigmund Freud Collection, Manuscript Division, Library of Congress, Washington, D.C., p. 33.
[13] "Freud's Theory of Hysteria: A Reply to Aschaffenburg," CW 4, § 16, tr. mod.
[14] "On the Psychology of Dementia Praecox: An Attempt," CW 3.

only by one who had applied the psychoanalytic method many times and who really investigates as Freud investigates. . . . He who does not or cannot do this should not pronounce judgement on Freud, else he acts like those famous men of science who disdained to look through Galileo's telescope. Fairness to Freud does not mean, as many fear, an unqualified submission to a dogma; one can very well maintain an independent judgement. If I, for instance, acknowledge the complex mechanisms of dreams and hysteria, this does not mean that I attribute to the infantile sexual trauma the exclusive importance that Freud apparently does. Still less does it mean that I place sexuality so predominantly in the foreground or even grant it the psychological universality which Freud, it seems, postulates under the impression of the certainly powerful role which sexuality plays in the psyche. Concerning Freudian therapy, it is in the best case one of the possible, and perhaps does not always offer what one theoretically expects.[15]

In 1909, before any book of Freud's, the work was translated, the first 'psychoanalytic' book in English. In their preface, Abraham Brill and Frederick Peterson wrote that Bleuler and Jung had "inaugurated a new epoch in psychiatry by attempting to penetrate into the mysteries of the individual influence of the symptoms."[16]

With the lead of Bleuler and Jung, the Burghölzli became the center of the psychoanalytic movement. In 1908, the *Jahrbuch für psychoanalytische und psychopathologische Forschungen* [Yearbook for Psychoanalytic and Psychopathological Researches] was established, with Bleuler and Jung as the editors. Due to their advocacy, psychoanalysis gained a hearing in the German psychiatric world. It is important to note that at this stage, psychoanalytic theory had not yet acquired the doctrinal fixity that it soon would. In correspondence with Freud, Jung set out his reservations on a number of points in Freud's theories, such as the sexual theory of the libido and the attempt to view the etiology of the psychoses purely psychogenically, and tried (unsuccessfully) to convince Freud to bring psychoanalytic theory into closer alignment with biology. At

[15] "On the Psychology of Dementia Praecox," *CW* 3, pp. 3–4, tr. mod.
[16] Brill and Peterson, "Translators' Preface," in Jung, *The Psychology of Dementia Praecox*, pp. v–vi.

this stage, Jung's divergences were tolerated within the framework of the wider political alliance.[17]

In 1909, on the occasion of the twentieth anniversary of Clark University, Jung was invited, along with Freud, to present some lectures at the university and receive an honorary degree. For American psychiatrists and psychologists, it would have been Jung, rather than Freud, who was the main draw.[18]

The following year, an international psychoanalytic association was formed, with Jung as the president. The movement was riven by dissensions and acrimonious disagreements.[19] Freud and his followers had been able to dismiss the views of his critics by arguing that they had never practiced his method. However, Freud was now faced with the situation that the most senior representatives of the movement were voicing views that were close to those of his critics, and their views could not be so easily dismissed. Toward the end of 1910, a conflict broke out between Freud and Alfred Adler, his most prominent follower in Vienna and president of the Vienna Psychoanalytical Society.[20] On 3 December 1910, Freud wrote to Jung: "The crux of the matter—and that is what really alarms me—is that [Adler] minimizes the sexual drive and our opponents will soon be able to speak of an experienced psychoanalyst whose conclusions are radically different from ours."[21] Freud's response was one of pathologization.[22] Adler was forced to resign, and in June 1911, he and his colleagues established a society for free psychoanalytic research. Later that autumn, the psychiatrist Hans Maier, who had succeeded Jung at the Burghölzli, was excluded from attending the Zurich Psychoanalytic Society. Follow-

---

[17] See Paul Stepansky, "The Empiricist as Rebel: Jung, Freud, and the Burdens of Discipleship," *Journal of the History of the Behavioral Sciences* 12, pp. 216–39.

[18] See Richard Skues, "Clark Revisited: Reappraising Freud in America," in John Burnham, ed., *After Freud Left: Centennial Reflections on His 1909 Visit to the United States* (Chicago: University of Chicago Press, 2012).

[19] On this period, see Mikkel Borch-Jacobsen and Sonu Shamdasani, *The Freud Files: An Inquiry into the History of Psychoanalysis* (Cambridge: Cambridge University Press, 2012); and George Makari, *Revolution in Mind: The Creation of Psychoanalysis* (New York: Harper Collins, 2008), chapter 7, "Integration/Disintegration."

[20] See Bernhard Handlbauer, *The Freud-Adler Controversy* (Oxford: Oneworld, 1998).

[21] William McGuire, ed., *The Freud/Jung Letters*, tr. R. Mannheim and R.F.C. Hull (Princeton, N.J.: Princeton University Press, 1974), p. 376.

[22] See Marina Leitner, "Pathologizing as a Way of Dealing with Conflicts and Dissent in the Psychoanalytic Movement," *Free Associations* 7, 3, 1999, pp. 459–83.

ing this episode, Bleuler resigned from the International Psycho-analytical Association.

In 1909, Jung resigned from the Burghölzli to devote himself to his growing private practice and his research interests. His retirement from the Burghölzli coincided with a shift in his research interests to the study of mythology, folklore, and religion, and he assembled a vast private library of scholarly works. These researches culminated in *Transformations and Symbols of the Libido*,[23] published in two installments in 1911 and 1912. In this work, Jung differentiated two kinds of thinking. Taking his cue from William James, among others, Jung contrasted directed thinking and fantasy thinking. The former was verbal and logical. The latter was passive, associative, and imagistic. The former was exemplified by science and the latter by mythology. Jung claimed that the ancients lacked a capacity for directed thinking, which was a modern acquisition. Fantasy thinking took place when directed thinking ceased. *Transformations and Symbols of the Libido* was an extended study of fantasy thinking, and of the continued presence of mythological themes in the dreams and fantasies of contemporary individuals. Jung reiterated the anthropological equation between the prehistoric, the primitive, and the child. He held that the elucidation of current-day fantasy thinking in adults would concurrently shed light on the thought of children, savages, and prehistoric peoples.[24]

In this work, Jung synthesized nineteenth-century theories of memory, heredity, and the unconscious and posited a phyloge-netic layer to the unconscious that was still present in everyone, consisting of mythological images. For Jung, myths were symbols of the libido, and they depicted its typical movements. He used the comparative method of anthropology to draw together a vast pan-oply of myths, and then subjected them to analytic interpretation. He later termed his use of the comparative method 'amplifica-tion.' He claimed that there had to be typical myths that corre-sponded to the ethnopsychological development of complexes. Following Jacob Burckhardt, Jung termed such typical myths 'pri-mordial images' ('Urbilder'). One particular myth was given a central role: that of the hero. For Jung, this represented the life of

[23] *CW* B.
[24] "The Psychology of the Unconscious," *CW* B, § 36. In his 1952 revision of this text, Jung qualified this ("Symbols of Transformation," *CW* 5, § 29).

the individual, attempting to become independent and to free himself from the mother. He interpreted the incest motif as an attempt to return to the mother to be reborn. He was later to herald this work as marking the discovery of the collective unconscious, though the term itself was of a later date.[25] It was in the second installment of the book that Jung explicitly set out his divergence with Freud's theory of the sexual libido and presented his own account of the development of the individual. The substance of Jung's critique is presented in detail in his New York lectures.

During the course of 1912, the personal relationship between Freud and Jung seriously deteriorated. On 20 August 1912, Freud wrote to James Jackson Putnam, "After the disgraceful defection of Adler, a gifted thinker but a malicious paranoiac, I am now in trouble with our friend, Jung, who apparently has not outgrown his own neurosis."[26] That summer, Ernest Jones proposed the formation of a secret committee to defend the cause of psychoanalysis "like the Paladins of Charlemagne."[27] Notably absent from this committee was Jung, then president of the International Psychoanalytical Association.

AUTUMN IN NEW YORK

At the beginning of 1912, Smith Ely Jelliffe had invited Jung to lecture in the new international extension course in medicine at Fordham University.[28] Jung's trip led to the postponement of the

[25] "Address on the Occasion of the Founding of the C. G. Jung Institute, Zurich, 24 April 1948," *CW* 18, § 1131.
[26] Nathan Hale, ed., *James Jackson Putnam and Psychoanalysis: Letters between Putnam and Sigmund Freud, Ernest Jones, William James, Sándor Ferenczi, and Morton Prince, 1877–1917* (Cambridge, Mass.: Harvard University Press, 1971), p. 146.
[27] Jones to Freud, 7 August 1912, in Andrew Paskauskas, ed., *The Complete Correspondence of Sigmund Freud and Ernest Jones, 1908–1939* (Cambridge, Mass.: Harvard University Press, 1993), p. 149. See Andrew Paskauskas, "Freud's Break with Jung: The Crucial Role of Ernest Jones," *Free Associations* 11, 1988, pp. 7–34. On the secret committee, see Gerhard Wittenberger, *Das "Geheime Komitee" Sigmund Freuds: Institionalisierungsprozesse in der Psychoanalytischen Bewegung zwischen 1912 und 1927* (Tübingen: Editions Diskord, 1995).
[28] Freud to Brill, 14 February 1912, Library of Congress, courtesy of Ernst Falzeder. To Ferenczi, Freud wrote on 23 June 1912: "Jung's 'summons to America' shouldn't be anything good. A little, unknown *Catholic* university run by Jesuits, which Jones had

congress of the International Psychoanalytical Association, which had been due to be held in the autumn.

On 13 May, Jung wrote to Jelliffe:

I accept your kind invitation to stay in your house during the time of my lectures. I am very grateful for this arrangement, because life in hotels in New York is somewhat disagreeable.

As I already told you, I hope to be in N. Y. on September 18 (Kaiser Wilhelm II).[29]

On 2 August, Jung informed Freud, "My American lectures are now finished and will contain various proposals for the modification of certain theoretical formulations. This step was difficult. I shall not however overcome my father following Adler's recipe, as you seem to suppose. This doesn't apply to me."[30] The lectures were translated into English by David Eder and Maria Moltzer.[31]

On 7 September, Jung left for New York, just as the second installment of *Transformations and Symbols of the Libido* appeared in the *Jahrbuch*. The period of suspension of criticism that he had indicated in his 1907 letter to Bezzola had now come to an end. Strikingly, in contrast to the convoluted arguments of *Transformations and Symbols of the Libido*, Jung then gave a very clear and lucid account of the development of psychoanalysis, together with his criticisms and reformulations of it. The ninth lecture presented an account of analysis of a child by Maria Moltzer, who was working as Jung's assistant. The lectures were attended by around ninety teachers and practitioners.

On 8 October, Jung gave a talk at the New York Academy of Medicine on "Psychoanalysis and Neurosis," which presented a summary of some of his revisions of psychoanalysis, and ended by

---

turned down." Eva Brabant, Ernst Falzeder, and Patrizia Giampieri-Deutsch, eds., *The Correspondence of Sigmund Freud and Sándor Ferenczi: Volume 1, 1908–1914*, tr. Peter Hoffer, with an introduction by André Haynal (Cambridge, Mass.: Harvard University Press, 2000), p. 387.

[29] John Burnham, *Jelliffe: American Psychoanalyst and Physician and His Correspondence with Sigmund Freud and C. G. Jung*, ed. William McGuire (Chicago: University of Chicago Press, 1983), p. 190.

[30] McGuire, *The Freud/Jung Letters*, p. 512, tr. mod. Hull omitted the second sentence in his translation.

[31] On Moltzer, see my *Cult Fictions: Jung and the Founding of Analytical Psychology* (London: Routledge, 1998); and my introduction to *The Red Book: Liber Novus* (New York: Norton, 2009) pp. 204–5.

noting that the views he was presenting concerning the etiology of the neuroses reconciled Freud's views with those of his great rival Pierre Janet, which would have been an anathema to the former.[32] He also gave two clinical lectures on dementia praecox at Bellevue Hospital in New York and at the New York State Psychiatric Institute at Ward's Island. James Jackson Putnam heard one of Jung's lectures and conveyed his impressions to Ernest Jones on 24 October:

> He seems to me a strong but egotistical man (if I may say this in complete confidence), and to be under the necessity of accentuating any peculiarity of his own position for his own personal satisfaction. I cannot think that any serious breach would be occasioned by this present movement on his part. . . . The point which seemed to me to indicate most strongly the idea of a breaking off on his part was that he said, if I understood him rightly, that he thought the significance of the whole conception of infantile sexual tendencies in Freud's sense had been overrated; that all persons, sick or well, have about the same fantasies, and that for example, he did not any longer believe that the sensations which a nursing child has could be classified as sexual in any sense, but only as related to nutritional necessities.[33]

After delivering the lectures, Jung went to St. Elizabeth's hospital at the invitation of William Alanson White. While there, he conducted some clinical investigations of 'Negroes' that convinced him that collective patterns were not only racially inherited, but universal.[34] He also visited Trigant Burrow in Baltimore and went to Chicago, and presented lectures in both cities. After returning to Switzerland, Jung was awarded an honorary degree in absentia. The Fordham Monthly noted:

> The degree of Doctor of Laws is conferred, in absentia, on Dr. Karl Jung, of the University of Zurich, Switzerland. Dr. Jung, though not yet in his forties, has attracted the attention of the world by his contributions to psycho-analysis, and

[32] "Psychoanalysis and Neurosis," *CW* 4, § 574.
[33] Hale, *James Jackson Putnam and Psychoanalysis*, p. 277.
[34] See my *Jung and the Making of Modern Psychology: The Dream of a Science* (Cambridge: Cambridge University Press, 2003), pp. 311–12.

above all by his demonstrations in word association, time reactions and the measurement of emotional stress. The value
of these discoveries in criminology are just coming to be
properly appreciated and their further significance is but a
matter of natural development. His studies in Dementia
Praecox attracted worldwide attention, and his monograph
on the subject published originally in German, but now available also in English and French, is one of the best known of
recent publications, particularly among the specialists in
neurology and psychiatry.[35]

On his return, Jung gave Freud an account of his lectures:

I gave 9 lectures at the Jesuit (!) University of Fordham, New
York—a critical account of the development of the theory of
ΨA. I had an audience of ca. 90 psychiatrists and neurologists. The lectures were in English. Besides that, I held a
2-hour seminar every day for a fortnight for ca. 8 professors.
Naturally I also made room for those of my views which deviate in places from the hitherto existing conceptions, particularly in regard to the libido theory. I found that my version of
ΨA won over many friends, who until now had been help-
lessly at a loss with the problem of the sexuality of the
neurosis.[36]

Jung's lectures were published in English in installments between
1913 and 1915 in the first volumes of the *Psychoanalytic Review,*
which had been founded by Jelliffe and White. They appeared as a
monograph in 1915 in the *Nervous and Mental Disease Monograph
Series,* his second book in English. Jung's revision of psychoanalysis
was taken on board by Jelliffe and White, and it can be argued that
it contributed to the rapid expansion of psychoanalysis in America
that took place at this time. In 1913, the lectures appeared in German in the *Jahrbuch* (of which Jung was shortly to resign as editor),
with some revisions, and then as a separate monograph.

Given Jung's status as president of the International Psychoanalytical Association and his international standing, the Freudians
were fearful concerning the impact of Jung's theoretical revisions,

[35] *The Fordham Monthly,* November 1912, p. 4.
[36] McGuire, *The Freud/Jung Letters,* p. 515, tr. mod.

as they moved so much closer to positions held by critics of psychoanalysis. On 25 April 1913, Jones wrote to Freud, "I am deeply impressed by the success of Jung's campaign, for he appeals to formidable prejudices. It is, in my opinion, the most critical period that Ψα will have to go through."[37]

Jung was under no illusions as to how his work would be received in the Freudian camp. On 15 November 1912, he wrote to Jones:

> Freud is convinced that I am thinking under the domination of a father complex against him and then all is complex-nonsense. . . . Against this insinuation I am completely helpless. . . . If Freud understands each attempt to think in a new way about the problems of psychoanalysis as a personal resistance, things become impossible.[38]

In the winter of 1912, Jung's communications with Freud broke down, and on 3 January 1913, Freud wrote to Jung ending their personal relationship.[39] It wasn't till the summer that Freud read Jung's New York lectures, and his private reaction was less critical than he himself had expected. He wrote to Ferenczi on 5 August:

> I have now read Jung's paper myself and find it good and innocuous, beyond my expectation. Jones is quite right with his criticism; the errors are palpable, the comparisons slanted; much that he presents in his aggressive tone as discovery is, moreover, congruent with our intellectual property; but the contradictions remain entirely on Ψα's ground. Much toward the end about therapy, transference, etc. is even excellent. What is stupid is his insistence on inertia as an etiological fac-

---

[37] Paskauskas, *The Complete Correspondence of Sigmund Freud and Ernest Jones, 1908–1939,* p. 199. On 14 November 1912, Jones reported to Freud a statement by Pierce Clark to James Jackson Putnam that "I think that Ψα in the light in which Jung formulates it is bound to have a very wide and rapid expansion from now on. It certainly removes some of the disagreeable barriers hitherto impeding the progress of the movement" (ibid., p. 176).

[38] Sigmund Freud Copyrights, Wivenhoe. On 14 April 1912, Freud had written to Binswanger apropos Jung, "Probably what is behind this is that he is playing out his father complex against me, for which I have certainly provided no cause, and if one pursued the matter one would probably find the influence of a woman, not his wife" (p. 83).

[39] McGuire, *The Freud/Jung Letters,* p. 539.

tor, instead of the Oedipus complex. . . . On the whole, I have very much overestimated the danger from a distance.[40]

It would be a mistake to consider Jung's theoretical differences with Freudian theory as leading to his break with Freud. Rather, the collapse of their personal relationship and the political alliance they had formed led to a situation where, in the public domain, theoretical differences were presented as rationalized justifications. Hence a concerted campaign of critical reviews against Jung's works was orchestrated by Freud; Karl Abraham and Ernest Jones wrote strident condemnations of Jung's New York lectures.[41]

THE AFTERMATH

In many respects, the fears of the Freudians concerning the success of Jung's reformulations proved to be well founded. In a comprehensive survey of the reception in the British press between 1912 and 1925, Dean Rapp showed that the works of Jung and his followers consistently received better reviews than the works of Freud and the psychoanalysts. Rapp states that the most frequent charge against Freud was that he had exaggerated the role of sexuality.[42] In the period between 1912 and 1919, Rapp notes that reviewers stated their preference for Jung's wider conception of the libido.[43] The reception of Jung's work in America—where it has had its deepest impact—has yet to be written.[44] But my impression, based on a survey of reviews in American publications during this period, particularly with regard to the reception of the 1916 En-

[40] Brabant et al., *The Correspondence of Sigmund Freud and Sándor Ferenczi: Volume 1, 1908–1914*, p. 505.

[41] Karl Abraham, in Hilda Abraham, ed., *Clinical Papers and Essays on Psychoanalysis*, tr. Hilda Abraham and D. R. Ellison (London: Hogarth Press, 1955), pp. 101–15; Ernest Jones, in *Internationale Zeitschrift für Ärztliche Psychoanalyse* 2, pp. 83–86.

[42] Dean Rapp, "The Reception of Freud by the British Press: General Interest and Literary Magazines, 1920–1925," *Journal of the History of the Behavioral Sciences* 24, 1988, p. 195.

[43] Dean Rapp, "The Early Discovery of Freud by the British General Educated Public, 1912–1919," *Social History of Medicine* 3, p. 233.

[44] For some initial indications, see John Burnham, *Psychoanalysis and American Medicine, 1894–1918: Medicine, Science and Culture* (New York: International Universities Press, 1967), pp. 128–29.

glish translation of Jung's *Transformations and Symbols of the Libido*, is that a similar trend also holds for his reception in America.[45] Many of the positions Jung articulated in these lectures became central tenets of later Jungian theory, and with the collapse of classical psychoanalytic theory, many in the psychoanalytic world today would have little problem with them. Jung's critique presented Freud with the need for a damage limitation exercise, which he performed through his own theoretical revisions.[46]

After delivering the lectures, Jung had some dreams that made a great impression upon him, and which were to take his work in a radically different direction,[47] and in the autumn of 1913, he commenced an intense period of self-investigation, at the center of which was his work on *Liber Novus*, *The Red Book*, which formed the basis of his later work.

In 1955, the German edition of these lectures was republished. In his preface to the reissue, Jung noted:

> It is a milestone on the long road of scientific endeavour, and so it shall remain. It may serve to call back to memory the constantly changing stages of the search in a newly discovered territory, whose boundaries are not marked out with any certainty even today, and thus to make its contribution to the story of an evolving science. I am therefore letting this book go to press again in its original form and with no essential alterations.[48]

These lectures were included in volume 4 of Jung's *Collected Works*, but this is their first republication in English as a separate monograph since 1915.

---

[45] See Beatrice Hinkle's press cutting book, Kristine Mann Library, New York.
[46] On this question, see Mikkel Borch-Jacobsen, *The Freudian Subject*, tr. Catherine Porter (Stanford, Calif.: Stanford University Press, 1988); and Ernst Falzeder, "Freud and Jung, Freudians and Jungians," paper presented at the Library of Congress Jung Symposium, 19 June 2011.
[47] See Jung, *Introduction to Jungian Psychology*, p. 40.
[48] *CW* 4, p. 87.

THE THEORY OF PSYCHOANALYSIS

[Written originally in German under the title *Versuch einer Darstellung der psychoanalytischen Theorie* and translated (by Dr. and Mrs. M. D. Eder and Miss Mary Moltzer) for delivery as a series of lectures under the present title at the medical school of Fordham University, New York, in September 1912. The German text was published in the *Jahrbuch für psychoanalytische und psychopathologische Forschungen* (Vienna and Leipzig), V (1913; reprinted as a book the same year); the English, in five issues of the *Psychoanalytic Review* (New York): I (1913/14): 1-4 and II (1915): 1. The latter was then republished in the Nervous and Mental Disease Monograph Series, No. 19 (New York, 1915). The analysis of a child in the last chapter had been previously presented as "Über Psychoanalyse beim Kinde" at the First International Congress of Pedagogy, Brussels, August 1911, and printed in the proceedings of the Congress (Brussels, 1912), II, 332-43.

[A second edition of the German text, with no essential alterations, was published in 1955 (Zurich). The present translation is made from this edition in consultation with the previous English version.

[The text of the 1913 and 1955 editions in German is uninterrupted by headings, but at the author's request the original division into nine lectures (ascertained from an examination of the manuscript) has here been preserved. This arrangement differs from that of the previous English version, which is divided into ten lectures; the chapter and section headings there introduced have in general been retained, with some modifications. A number of critical passages inserted at a later stage into the original manuscript and included in the German editions were omitted from the previous English version, together with the footnotes. In the present version these passages are given in pointed brackets ⟨ ⟩.
—EDITORS.]

FOREWORD TO THE FIRST EDITION

In these lectures I have attempted to reconcile my practical experiences in psychoanalysis with the existing theory, or rather, with the approaches to such a theory. It is really an attempt to outline my attitude to the guiding principles which my honoured teacher Sigmund Freud has evolved from the experience of many decades. Since my name is associated with psychoanalysis, and for some time I too have been the victim of the wholesale condemnation of this movement, it will perhaps be asked with astonishment how it is that I am now for the first time defining my theoretical position. When, some ten years ago, it came home to me what a vast distance Freud had already travelled beyond the bounds of contemporary knowledge of psychopathological phenomena, especially the psychology of complex mental processes, I did not feel in a position to exercise any real criticism. I did not possess the courage of those pundits who, by reason of their ignorance and incompetence, consider themselves justified in making "critical" refutations. I thought one must first work modestly for years in this field before one might dare to criticize. The unfortunate results of premature and superficial criticism have certainly not been lacking. Yet the great majority of the critics missed the mark as much with their indignation as with their technical ignorance. Psychoanalysis continued to flourish undisturbed and did not trouble itself about the unscientific chatter that buzzed around it. As everyone knows, this tree has waxed mightily, and not in one hemisphere only, but alike in Europe and America. Official critics meet with no better success than the Proktophantasmist in *Faust*, who laments in the Walpurgisnacht:

> Preposterous! You still intend to stay?
> Vanish at once! You've been explained away.

The critics have omitted to take it to heart that everything that exists has sufficient right to its own existence, and that this

3

holds for psychoanalysis as well. We will not fall into the error of our opponents, neither ignoring their existence nor denying their right to exist. But this enjoins upon us the duty of applying a just criticism ourselves, based on a proper knowledge of the facts. To me it seems that psychoanalysis stands in need of this weighing-up from inside.

It has been wrongly suggested that my attitude signifies a "split" in the psychoanalytic movement. Such schisms can only exist in matters of faith. But psychoanalysis is concerned with knowledge and its ever-changing formulations. I have taken as my guiding principle William James's pragmatic rule: "You must bring out of each word its practical cash-value, set it at work within the stream of your experience. It appears less as a solution, then, than as a program for more work, and more particularly as an indication of the ways in which existing realities may be changed. *Theories thus become instruments, not answers to enigmas, in which we can rest.* We don't lie back upon them, we move forward, and, on occasion, make nature over again by their aid." [1]

In the same way, my criticism does not proceed from academic arguments, but from experiences which have forced themselves on me during ten years of serious work in this field. I know that my own experience in no wise approaches Freud's quite extraordinary experience and insight, but nonetheless it seems to me that certain of my formulations do express the observed facts more suitably than Freud's version of them. At any rate I have found, in my teaching work, that the conceptions I have put forward in these lectures were of particular help to me in my endeavours to give my pupils an understanding of psychoanalysis. I am far indeed from regarding a modest and temperate criticism as a "falling away" or a schism; on the contrary, I hope thereby to promote the continued flowering and fructification of the psychoanalytic movement, and to open the way to the treasures of psychoanalytic knowledge for those who, lacking practical experience or handicapped by certain theoretical preconceptions, have so far been unable to master the method.

For the opportunity to deliver these lectures I have to thank my friend Dr. Smith Ely Jelliffe, of New York, who kindly in-

---

1 [*Pragmatism* (1907), p. 53.]

vited me to take part in the Extension Course at Fordham University, in New York. The nine lectures were given in September 1912. I must also express my best thanks to Dr. Gregory, of Bellevue Hospital, for his ready assistance at my clinical demonstrations.

Only after the preparation of these lectures, in the spring of 1912, did Alfred Adler's book *Über den nervosen Charakter* [*The Nervous Constitution*] become known to me, in the summer of that year. I recognize that he and I have reached similar conclusions on various points, but here is not the place to discuss the matter more thoroughly. This should be done elsewhere.

C. G. J.

Zurich, autumn 1912

FOREWORD TO THE SECOND EDITION

Since the appearance of the first edition in 1913 so much time has elapsed, and so many things have happened, that it is quite impossible to rework a book of this kind, coming from a long-past epoch and from one particular phase in the development of knowledge, and bring it up to date. It is a milestone on the long road of scientific endeavour, and so it shall remain. It may serve to call back to memory the constantly changing stages of the search in a newly discovered territory, whose boundaries are not marked out with any certainty even today, and thus to make its contribution to the story of an evolving science. I am therefore letting this book go to press again in its original form and with no essential alterations.

C. G. J.

October 1954

1. A REVIEW OF THE EARLY HYPOTHESES

203   It is no easy task to lecture on psychoanalysis at the present time. I am not thinking so much of the fact that this whole field of research raises—I am fully convinced—some of the most difficult problems facing present-day science. Even if we put this cardinal fact aside, there remain other serious difficulties which interfere considerably with the presentation of the material. I cannot offer you a well-established, neatly rounded doctrine elaborated from the practical and the theoretical side. Psychoanalysis has not yet reached that point of development, despite all the labour that has been expended upon it. Nor can I give you a description of its growth *ab ovo*, for you already have in your country, dedicated as always to the cause of progress, a number of excellent interpreters and teachers who have spread a more general knowledge of psychoanalysis among the scientifically-minded public. Besides this, Freud, the true discoverer and founder of the movement, has lectured in your country and given an authentic account of his views. I, too, have already had the great honour of lecturing in America, on the experimental foundation of the theory of complexes and the application of psychoanalysis to education.[1]

204   In these circumstances you will readily appreciate that I am afraid of repeating what has already been said or already been published in scientific journals. Another difficulty to be considered is the fact that quite extraordinary misconceptions prevail in many quarters concerning the nature of psychoanalysis. At times it is almost impossible to imagine what exactly these erroneous conceptions might be. But sometimes they are so preposterous that one is astonished that anyone with a scientific background could ever arrive at ideas so remote from reality. Obviously it would not be worth while to cite examples of these curiosities. It will be better to devote time and energy to discussing those problems of psychoanalysis which by their very nature give rise to misunderstandings.

1 [The Clark Lectures. See par. 154, n. 4, supra.—Editors.]

6

THE TRAUMA THEORY

205   Although it has been pointed out on any number of occasions before, many people still do not seem to know that the
theory of psychoanalysis has changed considerably in the course
of the years. Those, for instance, who have read only the first
book, *Studies on Hysteria*,[2] by Breuer and Freud, still believe
that, according to psychoanalysis, hysteria and the neuroses in
general are derived from a so-called trauma in early childhood.
They continue senselessly to attack this theory, not realizing
that it is more than fifteen years since it was abandoned and replaced by a totally different one. This change is of such great
importance for the whole development of the technique and
theory of psychoanalysis that we are obliged to examine it in
rather more detail. So as not to weary you with case histories
that by now are well known, I shall content myself with refer-
ring to those mentioned in Breuer and Freud's book, which I
may assume is known to you in its English translation. You will
there have read that case of Breuer's to which Freud referred in
his lectures at Clark University,[3] and will have discovered that
the hysterical symptom did not derive from some unknown
anatomical source, as was formerly supposed, but from certain
psychic experiences of a highly emotional nature, called traumata or psychic wounds. Nowadays, I am sure, every careful
and attentive observer of hysteria will be able to confirm from
his own experience that these especially painful and distressing
occurrences do in fact often lie at the root of the illness. This
truth was already known to the older physicians.

206   So far as I know, however, it was really Charcot who, probably influenced by Page's theory of "nervous shock," [4] first made
theoretical use of this observation. Charcot knew, from his experience of the new technique of hypnotism, that hysterical
symptoms can be produced and also be made to disappear by

2 [First published 1895; partially trans. by A. A. Brill in *Selected Papers on Hysteria and Other Neuroses* (New York, 1909; later edns.); trans. in Standard Edn.
of Freud, II (1955).—EDITORS.]
3 ["Five Lectures on Psycho-Analysis"; see par. 154, n. 4, supra.—EDITORS.]
4 [Probably Herbert W. Page, British psychiatrist, who published on this subject;
see Bibliography.—EDITORS.]

suggestion. He believed something of the kind could be observed in those increasingly common cases of hysteria caused by accidents. The traumatic shock would be comparable, in a sense, to the moment of hypnosis, since the emotion it produced would cause, temporarily, a complete paralysis of the will during which the trauma could become fixed as an auto-suggestion.

207   This conception laid the foundations for a theory of psychogenesis. It was left for later aetiological researches to find out whether the same mechanism, or a similar one, existed in cases of hysteria which could not be called traumatic. This gap in our knowledge of the aetiology of hysteria was filled by the discoveries of Breuer and Freud. They showed that even in cases of ordinary hysteria which had not been regarded as traumatically conditioned the same traumatic element could be found, and that it seemed to have an aetiological significance. So it was very natural for Freud, himself a pupil of Charcot, to see in this discovery a confirmation of Charcot's views. Consequently, the theory elaborated out of the experience of that period, mainly by Freud, bore the imprint of a traumatic aetiology. It was therefore fittingly called the trauma theory.

208   The new thing about this theory, apart from the truly admirable thoroughness of Freud's analysis of hysterical symptoms, is the abandonment of the concept of auto-suggestion, which was the dynamic element in the original theory. It was replaced by a more detailed conception of the psychological and psychophysical effects produced by the shock. The shock or trauma causes an excitation which, under normal conditions, is got rid of by being expressed ("abreacted"). In hysteria, however, the trauma is incompletely abreacted, and this results in a "retention of the excitation," or a "blocking of affect." The energy of the excitation, always lying ready *in potentia,* is transmuted into the physical symptoms by the mechanism of conversion. According to this view, the task of therapy was to release the accumulated excitation, thereby discharging the repressed and converted affects from the symptoms. Hence it was aptly called the "cleansing" or "cathartic" method, and its aim was to "abreact" the blocked affects. That stage of the analysis was therefore bound up fairly closely with the symptoms—one analysed the symptoms, or began the work of analysis with the symptoms, very much in contrast to the psychoanalytical tech-

nique employed today. The cathartic method and the theory on which it is based have, as you know, been taken over by other professional people, so far as they are interested in psychoanalysis at all, and have also found appreciative mention in the text-books.

209   Although the discoveries of Breuer and Freud are undoubtedly correct in point of fact, as can easily be proved by any case of hysteria, several objections can nevertheless be raised against the trauma theory. The Breuer-Freud method shows with wonderful clearness the retrospective connection between the actual symptom and the traumatic experience, as well as the psychological consequences which apparently follow of necessity from the original traumatic situation. All the same, some doubt arises as to the *aetiological* significance of the trauma. For one thing, the hypothesis that a neurosis, with all its complications, can be related to events in the past—that is, to some factor in the patient's predisposition—must seem doubtful to anyone who knows hysteria. It is the fashion nowadays to regard all mental abnormalities not of exogenous origin as consequences of hereditary degeneration, and not as essentially conditioned by the psychology of the patient and his environment. But this is an extreme view which fails to do justice to the facts. We know very well how to find the middle course in dealing with the aetiology of tuberculosis. There are undoubtedly cases of tuberculosis where the germ of the disease proliferates from early childhood in soil predisposed by heredity, so that even under the most favourable conditions the patient cannot escape his fate. But there are also cases where there is no hereditary taint and no predisposition, and yet a fatal infection occurs. This is equally true of the neuroses, where things will not be radically different from what they are in general pathology. An extreme theory about predisposition will be just as wrong as an extreme theory about environment.

THE CONCEPT OF REPRESSION

210   Although the trauma theory gave distinct prominence to the predisposition, even insisting that some past trauma is the *conditio sine qua non* of neurosis, Freud with his brilliant em-

9

piricism had already discovered, and described in the Breuer-Freud *Studies*, certain elements which bear more resemblance to an "environment theory" than to a "predisposition theory," though their theoretical importance was not sufficiently appreciated at the time. Freud had synthesized these observations in a concept that was to lead far beyond the limits of the trauma theory. This concept he called "repression." As you know, by "repression" we mean the mechanism by which a conscious content is displaced into a sphere outside consciousness. We call this sphere the unconscious, and we define it as the psychic element of which we are not conscious. The concept of repression is based on the repeated observation that neurotics seem to have the capacity for forgetting significant experiences or thoughts so thoroughly that one might easily believe they had never existed. Such observations are very common and are well known to anyone who enters at all deeply into the psychology of his patients.

211   As a result of the Breuer-Freud *Studies*, it was found that special procedures were needed to call back into consciousness traumatic experiences that had long been forgotten. This fact, I would mention in passing, is astonishing in itself, inasmuch as we are disinclined from the start to suppose that things of such importance could ever be forgotten. For this reason it has often been objected that the reminiscences brought back by hypnotic procedures are merely "suggested" and bear no relation to reality. Even if this doubt were justified, there would certainly be no justification for denying repression in principle on that account, for there are plenty of cases where the actual existence of repressed memories has been verified objectively. Quite apart from numerous proofs of this kind, it is possible to demonstrate this phenomenon experimentally, by the association test. Here we discover the remarkable fact that associations relating to feeling-toned complexes are much less easily remembered and are very frequently forgotten. As my experiments were never checked, this finding was rejected along with the rest. It was only recently that Wilhelm Peters, of the Kraepelin school, was able to confirm my earlier observations, proving that "painful experiences are very rarely reproduced correctly." [5]

5 ("Gefühl und Erinnerung," in Kraepelin, *Psychologische Arbeiten*, VI, pt. 2, p. 237.)

212   As you see, then, the concept of repression rests on a firm
empirical basis. But there is another side of the question that
needs discussing. We might ask if the repression is due to a
conscious decision of the individual, or whether the reminiscences disappear passively, without his conscious knowledge? In
Freud's writings you will find excellent proofs of the existence
of a conscious tendency to repress anything painful. Every psychoanalyst knows dozens of cases showing clearly that at some
particular moment in the past the patient definitely did not
want to think any longer of the content to be repressed. One
patient told me, very significantly: "Je l'ai mis de côté." On the
other hand, we must not forget that there are any number of
cases where it is impossible to show, even with the most careful
examination, the slightest trace of "putting aside" or of conscious repression, and where it seems as if the process of repression were more in the nature of a passive disappearance, or even
as if the impressions were dragged beneath the surface by some
force operating from below. Patients of the first type give us
the impression of being mentally well-developed individuals
who seem to suffer only from a peculiar cowardice in regard to
their own feelings. But among the second you may find cases
showing a more serious retardation of development, since here
the process of repression could be compared rather to an auto-
matic mechanism. This difference may be connected with the
question discussed above, concerning the relative importance
of predisposition and environment. Many factors in cases of the
first type appear to depend on the influence of environment and
education, whereas in the latter type the factor of predisposition
seems to predominate. It is pretty clear where the treatment will
be more effective.

213   As I have indicated, the concept of repression contains an
element which is in intrinsic contradiction with the trauma
theory. We saw, for instance, in the case of Miss Lucy R., analysed by Freud,[6] that the aetiologically significant factor was not
to be found in the traumatic scenes but in the insufficient readi-
ness of the patient to accept the insights that forced themselves
upon her. And when we think of the later formulation in the

6 [*Studies on Hysteria*, pp. 106ff.]

11

Schriften zur Neurosenlehre,[7] where Freud's experience obliged him to recognize certain traumatic events in early childhood as the source of the neurosis, we get a forcible impression of the incongruity between the concept of repression and that of the trauma. The concept of repression contains the elements of an aetiological theory of environment, while the trauma concept is a theory of predisposition.

214   At first the theory of neurosis developed entirely along the lines of the trauma concept. In his later investigations Freud came to the conclusion that no positive validity could be attributed to the traumatic experiences of later life, as their effects were conceivable only on the basis of a specific predisposition. It was evidently there that the riddle had to be solved. In pursuing the roots of hysterical symptoms, Freud found that the analytical work led back into childhood; the links reached backwards from the present into the distant past. The end of the chain threatened to get lost in the mists of earliest infancy. But it was just at that point that reminiscences appeared of certain sexual scenes—active or passive—which were unmistakably connected with the subsequent events leading to the neurosis. For the nature of these scenes you must consult the works of Freud and the numerous analyses that have already been published.

THE THEORY OF SEXUAL TRAUMA IN CHILDHOOD

215   Hence arose the theory of sexual trauma in childhood, which provoked bitter opposition not because of theoretical objections against the trauma theory in general, but against the element of sexuality in particular. In the first place, the very idea that children might be sexual, and that sexual thoughts might play any part in their lives, aroused great indignation. In the second place, the possibility that hysteria had a sexual basis was most unwelcome, for the sterile position that hysteria either was a uterine reflex-neurosis or arose from lack of sexual satisfaction

7 [By 1912, two volumes of Freud's *Sammlungen kleiner Schriften zur Neurosenlehre* had appeared, in 1906 and 1909 (another in 1913). The various contents of these volumes were trans., regrouped, in the *Collected Papers* (1924 ff.), and, further rearranged, in the Standard Edn. The precise reference here is unavailable.—EDITORS.]

had just been given up. Naturally, therefore, the validity of Freud's observations was contested. Had the critics confined themselves to that question, and not embellished their opposition with moral indignation, a calm discussion might have been possible. In Germany, for example, this method of attack made it impossible to gain any credit at all for Freud's theory. As soon as the question of sexuality was touched, it aroused universal resistance and the most arrogant contempt. But in reality there was only one question at issue: were Freud's observations true or not? That alone could be of importance to a truly scientific mind. I daresay his observations may seem improbable at first sight, but it is impossible to condemn them *a priori* as false. Wherever a really honest and thorough check has been carried out, the existence of the psychological connections established by Freud has been absolutely confirmed, but not the original hypothesis that it is always a question of real traumatic scenes.

216   Freud himself had to abandon that first formulation of his sexual theory of neurosis as a result of increasing experience. He could no longer retain his original view as to the absolute reality of the sexual trauma. Those scenes of a decidedly sexual character, the sexual abuse of children, and premature sexual activity in childhood were later on found to be to a large extent unreal. You may perhaps be inclined to share the suspicion of the critics that the results of Freud's analytical researches were therefore based on suggestion. There might be some justification for such an assumption if these assertions had been publicized by some charlatan or other unqualified person. But anyone who has read Freud's works of that period with attention, and has tried to penetrate into the psychology of his patients as Freud has done, will know how unjust it would be to attribute to an intellect like Freud's the crude mistakes of a beginner. Such insinuations only redound to the discredit of those who make them. Ever since then patients have been examined under conditions in which every possible precaution was taken to exclude suggestion, and still the psychological connections described by Freud have been proved true in principle. We are thus obliged to assume that many traumata in early infancy are of a purely fantastic nature, mere fantasies in fact, while others do have objective reality.

217   With this discovery, somewhat bewildering at first sight, the

13

aetiological significance of the sexual trauma in childhood falls to the ground, as it now appears totally irrelevant whether the trauma really occurred or not. Experience shows us that fantasies can be just as traumatic in their effects as real traumata. As against this, every doctor who treats hysteria will be able to recall cases where violent traumatic impressions have in fact precipitated a neurosis. This observation is only in apparent contradiction with the unreality, already discussed, of the infantile trauma. We know very well that there are a great many more people who experience traumata in childhood or adult life without getting a neurosis. Therefore the trauma, other things being equal, has no absolute aetiological significance and will pass off without having any lasting effect. From this simple reflection it is perfectly clear that the individual must meet the trauma with a quite definite inner predisposition in order to make it really effective. This inner predisposition is not to be understood as that obscure, hereditary disposition of which we know so little, but as a psychological development which reaches its climax, and becomes manifest, at the traumatic moment.

THE PREDISPOSITION FOR THE TRAUMA

218   I will now show you, by means of a concrete example, the nature of the trauma and its psychological preparation. It concerns the case of a young woman who suffered from acute hysteria following a sudden fright.[8] She had been to an evening party and was on her way home about midnight in the company of several acquaintances, when a cab came up behind them at full trot. The others got out of the way, but she, as though spellbound with terror, kept to the middle of the road and ran along in front of the horses. The cabman cracked his whip and swore; it was no good, she ran down the whole length of the road, which led across a bridge. There her strength deserted her, and to avoid being trampled on by the horses she would, in her desperation, have leapt into the river had not the passers-by restrained her. Now, this same lady had happened to be in St. Petersburg on the bloody 22nd of January [1905], in the very street which

8 [This case is fully reported in *Two Essays on Analytical Psychology*, pars. 8ff., 417ff.—Editors.]

14

was being cleared by the volleys of the soldiers. All round her people were falling to the ground dead or wounded; she, however, quite calm and clear-headed, espied a gate leading into a yard, through which she made her escape into another street. These dreadful moments caused her no further agitation. She felt perfectly well afterwards—indeed, rather better than usual.

219   This failure to react to an apparent shock is often observed. Hence it necessarily follows that the intensity of a trauma has very little pathogenic significance in itself; everything depends on the particular circumstances. Here we have a key to the "predisposition." We have therefore to ask ourselves: what are the particular circumstances of the scene with the cab? The patient's fear began with the sound of the trotting horses; for an instant it seemed to her that this portended some terrible doom —her death, or something as dreadful; the next moment she lost all sense of what she was doing.

220   The real shock evidently came from the horses. The patient's predisposition to react in so unaccountable a way to this unremarkable incident might therefore be due to the fact that horses have some special significance for her. We might conjecture, for instance, that she once had a dangerous accident with horses. This was actually found to be the case. As a child of about seven she was out for a drive with the coachman, when suddenly the horses took fright and at a wild gallop made for the precipitous bank of a deep river-gorge. The coachman jumped off and shouted to her to do likewise, but she was in such deadly fear that she could hardly make up her mind. Nevertheless she managed to jump in the nick of time, while the horses crashed with the carriage into the depths below. That such an event would leave a very deep impression hardly needs proof. Yet it does not explain why at a later date such an insensate reaction should follow a perfectly harmless stimulus. So far we know only that the later symptom had a prelude in childhood. The pathological aspect of it still remains in the dark.

221   This anamnesis, whose continuation we shall find out later,[9] shows very clearly the discrepancy between the so-called trauma and the part played by fantasy. In this case fantasy must predominate to a quite extraordinary degree in order to produce

9 [See infra, pars. 297ff. and 355ff.—EDITORS.]

such a great effect from so insignificant a stimulus. At first one is inclined to adduce that early childhood trauma as an explanation—not very successfully, it seems to me, because we still do not understand why the effects of that trauma remained latent so long, and why they manifested themselves precisely on this occasion and on no other. The patient must surely have had opportunities enough during her lifetime of getting out of the way of a carriage going at full speed. The moment of deadly peril she experienced earlier in St. Petersburg did not leave behind the slightest trace of neurosis, despite her being predisposed by the impressive event in her childhood. Everything about this traumatic scene has still to be explained, for, from the standpoint of the trauma theory, we are left completely in the dark.

222   You must forgive me if I return so persistently to this question of the trauma theory. I do not think it superfluous to do so, because nowadays so many people, even those closely connected with psychoanalysis, still cling to the old standpoint, and this gives our opponents, who mostly never read our writings or do so only very superficially, the impression that psychoanalysis still revolves round the trauma theory.

223   The question now arises: what are we to understand by this "predisposition," through which an impression, insignificant in itself, can produce such a pathological effect? This is a question of fundamental importance, and, as we shall see later, it plays a very important role in the whole theory of neurosis. We have to understand why apparently irrelevant events of the past still have so much significance that they can interfere in a daemonic and capricious way with our reactions in actual life.

THE SEXUAL ELEMENT IN THE TRAUMA

224   The early school of psychoanalysis, and its later disciples, did all they could to find in the special quality of those original traumatic experiences the reason for their later effectiveness. Freud went deepest: he was the first and only one to see that some kind of sexual element was mingled with the traumatic event, and that this admixture, of which the patient was generally unconscious, was chiefly responsible for the effect of the

trauma. The unconsciousness of sexuality in childhood seemed to throw a significant light on the problem of the long-lasting constellation caused by the original traumatic experience. The real emotional significance of that experience remains hidden all along from the patient, so that, not reaching consciousness, the emotion never wears itself out, it is never used up. We might explain the long-lasting constellative effect of the experience as a kind of *suggestion à échéance,* for this, too, is unconscious and develops its effect only at the appointed time.

225   It is hardly necessary to give detailed examples showing that the real character of sexual activities in infancy is not recognized. Doctors are aware, for instance, that open masturbation right up to adult life is not understood as such, especially by women. From this it is easy to deduce that a child would be even less conscious of the character of certain actions; hence the real meaning of these experiences remains hidden from consciousness even in adult life. In some cases the experiences themselves are completely forgotten, either because their sexual significance is quite unknown to the patient, or because their sexual character, being too painful, is not admitted, in other words, is repressed.

226   As already mentioned, Freud's observation that the admixture of a sexual element in the trauma is a characteristic concomitant having a pathological effect led to the theory of the infantile sexual trauma. This hypothesis means that the pathogenic experience is a sexual one.

INFANTILE SEXUAL FANTASY

227   At first this hypothesis was countered by the widespread opinion that children have no sexuality at all in early life, thus making such an aetiology unthinkable. The modification of the trauma theory already discussed, that the trauma is generally not real at all but essentially just fantasy, does not make things any better. On the contrary, it obliges us to see in the pathogenic experience a positive sexual manifestation of infantile fantasy. It is no longer some brutal accidental impression coming from outside, but a sexual manifestation of unmistakable clearness actually created by the child. Even real traumatic

17

experiences of a definitely sexual character do not happen to the child entirely without his co-operation; it was found that very often he himself prepares the way for them and brings them to pass. Abraham has furnished valuable proofs of great interest in support of this, which in conjunction with many other experiences of the same kind make it seem very probable that even real traumata are frequently aided and abetted by the psychological attitude of the child. Medical jurisprudence, quite independently of psychoanalysis, can offer striking parallels in support of this psychoanalytic assertion.

228   The precocious manifestations of sexual fantasy, and their traumatic effect, now seemed to be the source of the neurosis. One was therefore obliged to attribute to children a much more developed sexuality than was admitted before. Cases of precocious sexuality had long been recorded in the literature, for instance of a two-year-old girl who was menstruating regularly, or of boys between three and five years old having erections and therefore being capable of cohabitation. But these cases were curiosities. Great was the astonishment, therefore, when Freud began to credit children not only with ordinary sexuality but even with a so-called "polymorphous-perverse" sexuality, and moreover on the basis of the most exhaustive investigations. People were far too ready with the facile assumption that all this had merely been suggested to the patients and was accordingly a highly debatable artificial product.

229   In these circumstances, Freud's *Three Essays on the Theory of Sexuality* [10] provoked not only opposition but violent indignation. I need hardly point out that the progress of science is not furthered by indignation and that arguments based on the sense of moral outrage may suit the moralist—for that is his business—but not the scientist, who must be guided by truth and not by moral sentiments. If matters really are as Freud describes them, all indignation is absurd; if they are not, indignation will avail nothing. The decision as to what is the truth must be left solely to observation and research. In consequence of this misplaced indignation the opponents of psychoanalysis, with a few honourable exceptions, present a slightly comic picture of pitiful backwardness. Although the psychoanalytic school

10 [First published in 1905.]

18

was unfortunately unable to learn anything from its critics, as the critics did not trouble to examine our actual conclusions, and although it could not get any useful hints, because the psychoanalytic method of investigation was and still is unknown to them, it nevertheless remains the duty of our school to discuss very thoroughly the discrepancies between the existing views. It is not our endeavour to put forward a paradoxical theory contradicting all previous theories, but rather to introduce a certain category of new observations into science. We therefore consider it our duty to do whatever we can from our side to promote agreement. True, we must give up trying to reach an understanding with all those who blindly oppose us, which would be a waste of effort, but we do hope to make our peace with men of science. This will now be my endeavour in attempting to sketch the further conceptual development of psychoanalysis, up to the point where it reached the *sexual theory of neurosis*.[11]

[11] [See Ch. 4.—EDITORS.]

2. THE THEORY OF INFANTILE SEXUALITY

230   As you have heard in the last lecture, the discovery of precocious sexual fantasies, which seemed to be the source of the
neurosis, forced Freud to assume the existence of a richly developed infantile sexuality. As you know, the validity of this
observation has been roundly contested by many, who argue
that crude error and bigoted delusion have misled Freud and his
whole school, alike in Europe and in America, into seeing things
that never existed. We are therefore regarded as people in the
grip of an intellectual epidemic. I must confess that I have no
way of defending myself against this sort of "criticism." For the
rest, I must remark that science has no right to start off with
the idea that certain facts do not exist. The most one can say is
that they appear to be very improbable, and that more confirmation and more exact study are needed. This is also our reply to
the objection that nothing reliable can be learnt from the psychoanalytic method, as the method itself is absurd. No one believed in Galileo's telescope, and Columbus discovered America
on a false hypothesis. The method may for all I know be full of
errors, but that should not prevent its use. Chronological and
geographical observations were made in the past with quite inadequate instruments. The objections to the method must be
regarded as so many subterfuges until our opponents come to
grips with the facts. It is there that the issue should be decided
—not by a war of words.

231   Even our opponents call hysteria a psychogenic illness. We
believe we have discovered its psychological determinants and
we present, undaunted, the results of our researches for public
criticism. Anyone who does not agree with our conclusions is at
liberty to publish his own analyses of cases. So far as I know,
this has never yet been done, at least in the European literature.
Under these circumstances, critics have no right to deny our
discoveries *a priori*. Our opponents have cases of hysteria just
as we have, and these are just as psychogenic as ours, so there is
nothing to prevent them from finding the psychological deter-

minants. It does not depend on the method. Our opponents content themselves with attacking and vilifying our researches, but they do not know how to find a better way.

232   Many of our critics are more careful and more just, and admit that we have made many valuable observations and that the psychic connections revealed by the psychoanalytic method very probably hold good, but they maintain that our conception of them is all wrong. The alleged sexual fantasies of children, with which we are here chiefly concerned, must not be taken, they say, as real sexual functions, being obviously something quite different, since the specific character of sexuality is acquired only at the onset of puberty.

233   This objection, whose calm and reasonable tone makes a trustworthy impression, deserves to be taken seriously. It is an objection that has given every thoughtful analyst plenty of cause for reflection.

THE CONCEPT OF SEXUALITY

234   The first thing to be said about this problem is that the main difficulty resides in the concept of sexuality. If we understand sexuality as a fully developed function, then we must restrict this phenomenon to the period of maturity and are not justified in speaking of infantile sexuality. But if we limit our conception in this way, we are faced with a new and much greater difficulty. What name are we then to give to all those biological phenomena correlated with the sexual function in the strict sense, such as pregnancy, birth, natural selection, protection of offspring, and so on? It seems to me that all this belongs to the concept of sexuality, although a distinguished colleague did once say that childbirth is not a sexual act. But if these things do pertain to the concept of sexuality, then countless psychological phenomena must come into it too, for we know that an incredible number of purely psychological functions are connected with this sphere. I need only mention the extraordinary importance of fantasy in preparing and perfecting the sexual function. Thus we arrive at a highly biological conception of sexuality, which includes within it a series of psychological functions as well as a series of physiological phenomena. Availing

21

ourselves of an old but practical classification, we might identify sexuality with the instinct for the preservation of the species, which in a certain sense may be contrasted with the instinct of self-preservation.

235   Looking at sexuality from this point of view, we shall no longer find it so astonishing that the roots of the preservation of the species, on which nature sets such store, go much deeper than the limited conception of sexuality would ever allow. Only the more or less grown-up cat catches mice, but even the very young kitten at least plays at catching them. The puppy's playful attempts at copulation begin long before sexual maturity. We have a right to suppose that man is no exception to this rule. Even though we do not find such things on the surface in our well-brought-up children, observation of children of primitive peoples proves that they are no exceptions to the biological norm. It is really far more probable that the vital instinct for preservation of the species begins to unfold in early infancy than that it should descend at one fell swoop from heaven, fully-fledged, at puberty. Also, the organs of reproduction develop long before the slightest sign of their future function can be discerned.

236   So when the psychoanalytic school speaks of "sexuality," this wider concept of the preservation of the species should be associated with it, and it should not be thought that we mean merely the physical sensations and functions which are ordinarily connoted by that word. It might be said that in order to avoid misunderstandings one should not call the preliminary phenomena of early infancy "sexual." But this demand is surely not justified, since anatomical nomenclature is taken from the fully-developed system and it is not usual to give special names to the more or less rudimentary stages.

IMPORTANCE OF THE NUTRITIVE FUNCTION

237   Now although no fault can be found with Freud's sexual terminology as such, since he logically gives all the stages of sexual development the general name of sexuality, it has nevertheless led to certain conclusions which in my view are untenable. For if we ask ourselves how far the first traces of sexuality

go back into childhood, we have to admit that though sexuality exists implicity *ab ovo* it only manifests itself after a long period of extra-uterine life. Freud is inclined to see even in the infant's sucking at its mother's breast a kind of sexual act. He was bitterly attacked for this view, yet we must admit that it is sensible enough if we assume with Freud that the instinct for the preservation of the species, i.e., sexuality, exists as it were separately from the instinct of self-preservation, i.e., the nutritive function, and accordingly undergoes a special development *ab ovo*. But this way of thinking seems to me inadmissible biologically. It is not possible to separate the two modes of manifestation or functioning of the hypothetical life-instinct and assign each of them a special path of development. If we judge by what we see, we must take into consideration the fact that in the whole realm of organic nature the life-process consists for a long time only in the functions of nutrition and growth. We can observe this very clearly indeed in many organisms, for instance in butterflies, which as caterpillars first pass through an asexual stage of nutrition and growth only. The intra-uterine period of human beings, as well as the extra-uterine period of infancy, belong to this stage of the life process.

238   *This period is characterized by the absence of any sexual function,* so that to speak of manifest sexuality in infancy would be a contradiction in terms. The most we can ask is whether, among the vital functions of the infantile period, there are some that do not have the character of nutrition and growth and hence could be termed sexual. Freud points to the unmistakable excitement and satisfaction of the infant while sucking, and he compares these emotional mechanisms with those of the sexual act. This comparison leads him to assume that the act of sucking has a sexual quality. Such an assumption would be justifiable only if it were proved that the tension of a physical need, and its release by gratification, is a sexual process. But the fact that sucking has this emotional mechanism proves just the contrary. Consequently we can only say that this emotional mechanism is found both in the nutritive function and in the sexual function. If Freud derives the sexual quality of the act of sucking from the analogy of the emotional mechanism, biological experience would also justify a terminology qualifying the sexual act as a function of nutrition. This is exceeding the bounds in both

23

directions. What is quite evident is that the act of sucking cannot be qualified as sexual.

239   We know, however, of other functions at the infantile stage which apparently have nothing to do with the function of nutrition, such as sucking the finger and its numerous variants. Here is rather the place to ask whether such things belong to the sexual sphere. They do not serve nutrition, but produce pleasure. Of that there can be no doubt, but it nevertheless remains disputable whether the pleasure obtained by sucking should be called by analogy a sexual pleasure. It could equally well be called a nutritive pleasure. This latter qualification is the more apt in that the form of pleasure and the place where it is obtained belong entirely to the sphere of nutrition. The hand which is used for sucking is being prepared in this way for the independent act of feeding in the future. That being so, surely no one will beg the question by asserting that the first expressions of human life are sexual.

240   Yet the formula we hit on just now, that pleasure is sought in sucking the finger without serving any nutritive purpose, leaves us feeling doubtful whether it does belong entirely to the sphere of nutrition. We notice that the so-called bad habits of a child as it grows up are closely connected with early infantile sucking, like putting the finger in the mouth, biting the nails, picking the nose, ears, etc. We see, too, how easily these habits pass over into masturbation later on. The conclusion that these infantile habits are the first stages of masturbation or of similar activities, and therefore have a distinctly sexual character, cannot be denied: it is perfectly legitimate. I have seen many cases in which an indubitable correlation existed between these childish habits and masturbation, and if masturbation occurs in late childhood, before puberty, it is nothing but a continuation of the infantile bad habits. The inference from masturbation that other infantile habits have a sexual character appears natural and understandable from this point of view, in so far as they are acts for obtaining pleasure from one's own body.

241   From here it is but a short step to qualifying the infant's sucking as sexual. Freud, as you know, took that step and you have just heard me reject it. For here we come upon a contradiction which is very hard to resolve. It would be fairly easy if we could assume two separate instincts existing side by side.

Then the act of sucking the breast would be a nutritive act and at the same time a sexual act, a sort of combination of the two instincts. This seems to be Freud's conception. The obvious co-existence of the two instincts, or rather their manifestation in the form of hunger and the sexual drive, is found in the life of adults. But at the infantile stage we find *only* the function of nutrition, which sets a premium on pleasure and satisfaction. Its sexual character can be argued only by a *petitio principii*, for the facts show that the act of sucking is the first to give pleasure, not the sexual function. *Obtaining pleasure is by no means identical with sexuality.* We deceive ourselves if we think that the two instincts exist side by side in the infant, for then we project into the psyche of the child an observation taken over from the psychology of adults. The co-existence or separate manifestation of the two instincts is *not* found in the infant, for one of the instinctual systems is not developed at all, or is quite rudimentary. If we take the attitude that the striving for pleasure is something sexual, we might just as well say, paradoxically, that hunger is a sexual striving, since it seeks pleasure by satisfaction. But if we juggle with concepts like that, we should have to allow our opponents to apply the terminology of hunger to sexuality. This kind of one-sidedness appears over and over again in the history of science. I am not saying this as a reproach: on the contrary, we must be glad that there are people who are courageous enough to be immoderate and one-sided. It is to them that we owe our discoveries. What is regrettable is that each should defend his one-sidedness so passionately. Scientific theories are merely suggestions as to how things might be observed.

242   The co-existence of two instinctual systems is an hypothesis that would certainly facilitate matters, but unfortunately it is impossible because it contradicts the observed facts and, if pursued, leads to untenable conclusions.

THE POLYMORPHOUS-PERVERSE SEXUALITY OF INFANCY

243   Before I try to resolve this contradiction, I must say something more about Freud's sexual theory and the changes it has undergone. As I explained earlier, the discovery of a sexual

fantasy-activity in childhood, which apparently had the effect of a trauma, led to the assumption that the child must have, in contradiction to all previous views, an almost fully developed sexuality, and even a polymorphous-perverse sexuality. Its sexuality does not seem to be centred on the genital function and on the other sex, but is occupied with the child's own body, whence it is said to be autoerotic. If its sexual interest is directed outwards to another person, it makes but little difference to the child what that person's sex is. Hence the child may very easily be "homosexual." Instead of the non-existent, localized sexual function there are a number of so-called bad habits, which from this point of view appear as perverse actions since they have close analogies with subsequent perversions.

244   As a result of this conception sexuality, ordinarily thought of as a unity, was decomposed into a plurality of separate drives; and since it was tacitly assumed that sexuality originates in the genitals, Freud arrived at the conception of "erogenous zones," by which he meant the mouth, skin, anus, etc.

245   The term "erogenous zone" reminds us of "spasmogenic zone." At all events the underlying idea is the same: just as the spasmogenic zone is the place where a spasm originates, the erogenous zone is the place from which comes an afflux of sexuality. On the underlying model of the genitals as the anatomical source of sexuality, the erogenous zones would have to be conceived as so many genital organs out of which sexuality flows. This state is the polymorphous-perverse sexuality of children. The term "perverse" appeared justified by the close analogy with later perversions which are, so to speak, simply a new edition of certain "perverse" interests in early infancy. They are frequently connected with one or other of the erogenous zones and cause those sexual anomalies which are so characteristic of children.

SEXUAL COMPONENTS AS ENERGIC MANIFESTATIONS

246   From this point of view the later, normal, "monomorphic" sexuality is made up of several components. First it falls into a homo- and a heterosexual component, then comes the autoerotic component, and then the various erogenous zones. This concep-

tion can be compared with the position of physics before Robert Mayer, when only separate fields of phenomena existed, each credited with elementary qualities whose correlation was not properly understood. The law of the conservation of energy brought order into the relationship of forces to one another, at the same time abolishing the conception of those forces as having an absolute, elementary character and making them manifestations of the same energy. The same thing will have to happen with this splitting of sexuality into the polymorphous-perverse sexuality of childhood.

247   Experience compels us to postulate a constant interchange of individual components. It was recognized more and more that perversions, for instance, exist at the expense of normal sexuality, and that increased application of one form of sexuality follows a decrease in the application of another form. To make the matter clearer I will give an example. A young man had a homosexual phase lasting for some years, during which time he had no interest in girls. This abnormal condition gradually changed towards his twentieth year, and his erotic interests became more and more normal. He began to take an interest in girls, and soon he had overcome the last traces of homosexuality. This lasted for several years, and he had a number of successful love-affairs. Then he wanted to marry. But here he suffered a severe disappointment, as the girl he adored threw him over. During the ensuing phase he gave up all idea of marriage. After that he experienced a dislike of all women, and one day he discovered that he had become homosexual again, for young men once more had a peculiarly irritating effect upon him.

248   If we regard sexuality as consisting of a fixed heterosexual and a fixed homosexual component we shall never explain this case, since the assumption of fixed components precludes any kind of transformation. In order to do justice to it, we must assume a great mobility of the sexual components, which even goes so far that one component disappears almost completely while the other occupies the foreground. If nothing but a change of position took place, so that the homosexual component lapsed in full force into the unconscious, leaving the field of consciousness to the heterosexual component, modern scientific knowledge would lead us to infer that equivalent effects would then arise from the unconscious sphere. These effects would have to

be regarded as resistances to the activity of the heterosexual component, that is, as resistances against women. But in our case there is no evidence of this. Though faint traces of such influences existed, they were of such slight intensity that they could not be compared with the previous intensity of the homosexual component.

249   On the existing theory, it remains incomprehensible how the homosexual component, regarded as so firmly fixed, could disappear without leaving any active traces behind it. ⟨Further, it would be very difficult to conceive how these transformations come about. One could, at a pinch, understand the development passing through a homosexual stage in the pubertal period in order to lay the foundation for normal heterosexuality later, in a fixed, definite form. But how are we then to explain that the product of a gradual development, to all appearances bound up very closely with organic processes of maturation, is suddenly abolished under the impact of an impression, so as to make room for an earlier stage? Or, if two active components are postulated as existing simultaneously side by side, why is only one of them active and not the other as well? One might object that the homosexual component in men does in fact show itself most readily in a peculiar irritability, a special sensitiveness in regard to other men. According to my experience the apparent reason for this characteristic behaviour, of which we find so many examples in society today, is an invariable disturbance in the relationship with women, a special form of dependence on them. This would constitute the "plus" that is counterbalanced by the "minus" in the homosexual relationship. (Naturally this is not the real reason. The real reason is the infantile state of the man's character.)⟩

250   It was, therefore, urgently necessary to give an adequate explanation of such a change of scene. For this we need a dynamic hypothesis, since these permutations of sex can only be thought of as dynamic or energic processes. Without an alteration in the dynamic relationships, I cannot conceive how a mode of functioning can disappear like this. Freud's theory took account of this necessity. His conception of components, of separate modes of functioning, began to be weakened, at first more in practice than in theory, and was eventually replaced by a conception of energy. The term chosen for this was *libido*.

3. THE CONCEPT OF LIBIDO

251   Freud had already introduced the concept of libido in his *Three Essays on the Theory of Sexuality,* where he says:

> The fact of the existence of sexual needs in human beings and animals is expressed in biology by the assumption of a "sexual instinct," on the analogy of the instinct of nutrition, that is of hunger. Everyday language possesses no counterpart to the word "hunger," but science makes use of the word "libido" for that purpose.[1]

252   In Freud's definition the term *libido* connotes an exclusively sexual need, hence everything that Freud means by libido must be understood as sexual need or sexual desire. In medicine the term *libido* is certainly used for sexual desire, and specifically for sexual lust. But the classical use of the word as found in Cicero, Sallust, and others was not so exclusive; there it is used in the more general sense of passionate desire.[2] I mention this fact now, because further on it will play an important part in our argument, and because it is important to know that the term *libido* really has a much wider range of meaning than it has in medicine.

253   The concept of libido—whose sexual meaning in the Freudian sense we shall try to retain as long as possible—represents that dynamic factor which we were seeking in order to explain the shifting of the psychological scenery. This concept makes it much easier to formulate the phenomena in question. Instead of the incomprehensible exchanging of the homosexual component for the heterosexual component, we can now say that the libido was gradually withdrawn from its homosexual application and that it passed over in the same measure to a heterosexual application. In the process the homosexual component disappeared almost completely. It remained only an empty possibility, signifying nothing in itself. Its very existence is quite

1 [Standard Edn., VII, p. 135.]
2 [Cf. the definition of libido in *Symbols of Transformation,* pars. 185f.]

rightly denied by the layman, just as he would deny the possibility that he is a murderer. The libido concept also helps to explain the reciprocal relationships between the various modes of sexual functioning. At the same time, it does away with the original idea of a plurality of sexual components, which savoured too much of the old philosophical notion of psychic faculties. Their place is taken by libido, which is capable of the most varied applications. The earlier "components" represent only possible modes of action. The libido concept puts in the place of a divided sexuality split into many roots a dynamic unity, lacking which these once-significant components remain nothing but potential activities. This conceptual development is of the greatest importance; it accomplishes for psychology the same advance that the concept of energy introduced into physics. Just as the theory of the conservation of energy deprived the various forces of their elementary character and made them manifestations of a single energy, so the theory of libido deprives the sexual components of their elementary significance as psychic "faculties" and gives them a merely phenomenological value.

THE ENERGIC THEORY OF LIBIDO

254   This view is a far better reflection of reality than the theory of components. With the libido theory we can easily explain the case of the young man cited earlier. The disappointment he met with at the moment he wanted to marry drove his libido away from its heterosexual mode of application, with the result that it assumed a homosexual form again and thus reinduced the earlier homosexuality. Here I cannot refrain from remarking that the analogy with the law of the conservation of energy is very close. In both cases one has to ask, when one sees that a quantum of energy has disappeared, where this energy has re-emerged in the meantime? If we apply this point of view as an explanatory principle to the psychology of human conduct, we shall make the most surprising discoveries. We can then see that the most heterogeneous phases in an individual's psychological development are connected with one another in an energic relationship. Every time we come across a person who has a "bee in his bonnet," or a morbid conviction, or some extreme

attitude, we know that there is too much libido, and that the excess must have been taken from somewhere else where, consequently, there is too little. From this point of view psychoanalysis is a method which helps us to discover those places or functions where there is too little libido, and to restore the balance. Thus the symptoms of a neurosis must be regarded as exaggerated functions over-invested with libido.[3] The energy used for this purpose has been taken from somewhere else, and it is the task of the psychoanalyst to discover the place it was taken from or where it was never applied.

255   The question has to be reversed in the case of those syndromes characterized mainly by lack of libido, for instance apathetic states. Here we have to ask, where did the libido go? The patient gives us the impression of having no libido, and there are many doctors who take him at his face value. Such doctors have a primitive way of thinking, like a savage who, seeing an eclipse of the sun, believes that the sun has been swallowed and killed. But the sun is only hidden, and so it is with these patients. The libido is there, but it is not visible and is inaccessible to the patient himself. Superficially, we have here a lack of libido. It is the task of psychoanalysis to search out that hidden place where the libido dwells and where the patient himself cannot get at it. The hidden place is the "non-conscious," which we may also call the "unconscious" without attributing to it any mystical significance.

UNCONSCIOUS FANTASY SYSTEMS

256   Psychoanalysis has taught us that there are non-conscious psychological systems which, by analogy with conscious fantasies, can be described as unconscious fantasy systems. In states of neurotic apathy these unconscious fantasy systems are the objects of libido. We are fully aware that when we speak of unconscious fantasy-systems we are speaking only figuratively. By this we mean no more than that we accept as a necessary postulate the conception of psychic entities outside consciousness. Experience teaches us, we might say daily, that there are non-conscious

3 We meet with a similar view in Janet.

psychic processes which perceptibly influence the libido economy. Those cases known to every psychiatrist, in which a complicated system of delusions breaks out with comparative suddenness, prove that there must be unconscious psychic developments that have prepared the ground, for we can hardly suppose that such things come into being just as suddenly as they enter consciousness.

257   I have allowed myself to make this digression concerning the unconscious in order to point out that, with regard to the changing localization of libidinal investments, we have to reckon not merely with the conscious but with another factor, the unconscious, into which the libido sometimes disappears. We can now resume our discussion of the further consequences resulting from the adoption of the libido theory.

THE CONSERVATION OF LIBIDO

258   Freud has taught us, and we see it in the everyday practice of psychoanalysis, that there exist in early childhood, instead of the later normal sexuality, the beginnings of many tendencies which in later life are called "perversions." We have had to admit Freud's right to apply a sexual terminology to these tendencies. Through the introduction of the libido concept, we see that in adults those elementary components which seemed to be the origin and source of normal sexuality lose their importance and are reduced to mere potentialities. Their operative principle, their vital force, so to speak, is the libido. Without libido these components mean practically nothing. Freud, as we saw, gives the libido an unquestionably sexual connotation, something like "sexual need." It is generally assumed that libido in this sense comes into existence only at puberty. How, then, are we to explain the fact that children have a polymorphous-perverse sexuality, and that the libido activates not merely one perversion but several? If the libido, in Freud's sense, comes into existence only at puberty, it cannot be held accountable for earlier infantile perversions—unless we regard them as "psychic faculties," in accordance with the theory of components. Quite apart from the hopeless theoretical confusion this would lead to, we would be sinning against the methodological axiom

that "explanatory principles are not to be multiplied beyond the necessary."

259   There is no alternative but to assume that before and after puberty it is the same libido. Hence the infantile perversions arise in exactly the same way as in adults. Common sense will object to this, as obviously the sexual needs of children cannot possibly be the same as those of sexually mature persons. We might, however, compromise on this point and say with Freud that though the libido before and after puberty is the same it is different in its intensity. Instead of the intense sexual need after puberty there would be only a slight sexual need in childhood, gradually diminishing in intensity until, at about the first year, it is nothing but a trace. We could declare ourselves in agreement with this from the biological point of view. But we should also have to assume that everything that comes within the realm of the wider concept of sexuality discussed in the previous lecture is already present in miniature, including all those emotional manifestations of psychosexuality, such as need for affection, jealousy, and many other affective phenomena, and by no means least the neuroses of childhood. It must be admitted, however, that these affective phenomena in children do not at all give the impression of being "in miniature"; on the contrary, they can rival in intensity those of an adult. Nor should we forget that, as experience has shown, the perverse manifestations of sexuality in childhood are often more glaring, and even seem to be more richly developed, than in adults. In an adult showing a similar state of richly developed perversion we could rightly expect a total extinction of normal sexuality and of many other important forms of biological adaptation, as is normally the case with children. An adult is rightly called perverse when his libido is not used for normal functions, and the same can reasonably be said of a child: he is polymorphous-perverse because he does not yet know the normal sexual function.

260   These considerations suggest that perhaps the amount of libido is always the same and that no enormous increase occurs at sexual maturity. This somewhat audacious hypothesis leans heavily, it is clear, on the law of the conservation of energy, according to which the amount of energy remains constant. It is conceivable that the peak of maturity is reached only when the infantile, subsidiary applications of libido gradually discharge

33

themselves into one definite channel of sexuality and are extinguished in it. For the moment we must content ourselves with these suggestions, for we must next pay attention to one point of criticism concerning the nature of the infantile libido.

261   Many of our critics do not concede that the infantile libido is simply less intense but of essentially the same nature as the libido of adults. The libidinal impulses of adults are correlated with the genital function, those of children are not, or only in exceptional cases, and this gives rise to a distinction whose importance must not be underestimated. It seems to me that this objection is justified. There is indeed a considerable difference between immature and fully developed functions, just as there is between play and seriousness, between shooting with blank and with loaded cartridges. This would give the infantile libido that undeniably harmless character which is demanded by common sense. But neither can one deny that blank-shooting is shooting. We must get accustomed to the idea that sexuality really exists, even before puberty, right back into early childhood, and we have no grounds for not calling the manifestations of this immature sexuality sexual.

262   This naturally does not invalidate the objection which, while admitting the existence of infantile sexuality in the form we have described, nevertheless contests Freud's right to designate as "sexual" early infantile phenomena such as sucking. We have already discussed the reasons which may have induced Freud to stretch his sexual terminology so far. We mentioned, too, how this very act of sucking could be conceived just as well from the standpoint of the nutritive function and that, on biological grounds, there was actually more justification for this derivation than for Freud's view. It might be objected that these and similar activities of the oral zone reappear in later life in an undoubtedly sexual guise. This only means that these activities can be used later for sexual purposes, but proves nothing about their originally sexual character. I must, therefore, admit that I can find no ground for regarding the pleasure-producing activities of the infantile period from the standpoint of sexuality, but rather grounds to the contrary. It seems to me, so far as I am capable of judging these difficult problems correctly, that from the standpoint of sexuality it is necessary to divide human life into three phases.

34

THE THREE PHASES OF LIFE

263   The first phase embraces the first years of life; I call this
period the *presexual stage*.[4] It corresponds to the caterpillar
stage of butterflies, and is characterized almost exclusively by
the functions of nutrition and growth.

264   The second phase embraces the later years of childhood up
to puberty, and might be called the *prepubertal stage*. Ger-
mination of sexuality takes place at this period.

265   The third phase is the adult period from puberty on, and
may be called the period of *maturity*.

266   It will not have escaped you that the greatest difficulty lies
in assigning limits to the presexual stage. I am ready to confess
my great uncertainty in regard to this problem. When I look
back on my own psychoanalytic experiences with children—insufficiently numerous as yet, unfortunately—at the same time
bearing in mind the observations made by Freud, it seems to me
that the limits of this phase lie between the third and fifth year,
subject, of course, to individual variation. This age is an important one in many respects. The child has already outgrown
the helplessness of a baby, and a number of important psychological functions have acquired a reliable hold. From this period
on, the profound darkness of the early infantile amnesia, or dis-
continuity of consciousness, begins to be illuminated by the
sporadic continuity of memory. It seems as if, at this stage, an
essential step forward is taken in the emancipation and cen-
tring of the new personality. So far as we know, the first signs
of interests and activities which may fairly be called sexual also
fall into this period, even though these indications still have the
infantile characteristics of harmlessness and naïveté.

THE SEXUAL TERMINOLOGY

267   I think I have sufficiently explained why a sexual terminology cannot be applied to the presexual stage, so we may now
consider the other problems from the standpoint we have just

4 [Cf. *Symbols of Transformation,* par. 206.]

reached. You will remember that we dropped the problem of decreased libido in childhood because it was impossible in that way to reach any clear conclusion. We now take up this question once again, if only to see whether the energic conception fits in with our present formulations.

268   We saw that the difference between infantile and mature sexuality can be explained, according to Freud, by the diminishing intensity of sexuality in childhood. But we have just advanced reasons why it seems doubtful that the life-processes of a child, with the exception of sexuality, are any less intense than those of adults. We could say that, sexuality excepted, the affective phenomena, and the nervous symptoms if there are any, are quite as intense as in adults. Yet, on the energic view, they are all manifestations of libido. It is therefore difficult to believe that the intensity of libido can make the difference between mature and immature sexuality. Rather the difference seems to be conditioned by a change in the localization of libido (if such an expression be permitted). In contradistinction to its medical definition, the libido of a child is occupied far more with subsidiary functions of a mental and physical nature than with local sexual functions. This being so, one is tempted to withdraw the predicate "sexualis" from the term "libido" and to strike out the sexual definition of libido given in Freud's *Three Essays on the Theory of Sexuality*. The necessity for this becomes really urgent when we ask ourselves whether the intense joys and sorrows of a child in the first years of his life, that is, *at the presexual stage,* are conditioned solely by his sexual libido.

269   Freud has pronounced himself in favour of this supposition. There is no need for me to repeat here the reasons which compelled me to postulate a presexual stage. The caterpillar stage possesses an alimentary libido but no sexual libido; we have to put it like that if we want to retain the energic view which the libido theory offers us. I think there is nothing for it but to abandon the sexual definition of libido, or we shall lose what is valuable in the libido theory, namely the energic point of view. For a long time now the need to give the concept of libido breathing-space and to remove it from the narrow confines of the sexual definition has forced itself on the psychoanalytical school. One never wearied of insisting that sexuality was not to

be taken too literally but in a wider sense; yet exactly *how* remained obscure and so could not satisfy the serious critics.

271   I do not think I am going astray if I see the real value of the concept of libido not in its sexual definition but in its energic view, thanks to which we are in possession of an extremely valuable heuristic principle. We are also indebted to the energic view for dynamic images and correlations which are of inestimable value to us in the chaos of the psychic world. Freudians would be wrong not to listen to those critics who accuse our libido theory of mysticism and unintelligibility. We were deceiving ourselves when we believed that we could make the *libido sexualis* the vehicle of an energic conception of psychic life, and if many of Freud's school still believe that they are in possession of a well-defined and, so to speak, concrete conception of libido, they are not aware that this concept has been put to uses which far exceed the bounds of any sexual definition. Consequently the critics are right when they object that the libido theory purports to explain things which do not properly belong to its sphere. This really does evoke the impression that we are operating with a mystical entity.

THE PROBLEM OF LIBIDO IN DEMENTIA PRAECOX

271   In my book *Wandlungen und Symbole der Libido* I tried to furnish proof of these transgressions and at the same time to show the need for a new conception of libido which took account only of the energic view. Freud himself was forced to admit that his original conception of libido might possibly be too narrow when he tried to apply the energic view consistently to a famous case of dementia praecox—the so-called Schreber case.[5] This case is concerned among other things with that well-known problem in the psychology of dementia praecox, the loss of adaptation to reality, a peculiar phenomenon consisting in the special tendency of these patients to construct an inner fantasy world of their own, surrendering for this purpose their adaptation to reality.

272   One aspect of this phenomenon, the absence of emotional

[5] ["Psycho-Analytic Notes on an Autobiographical Account of a Case of Paranoia (Dementia Paranoides)."]

37

rapport, will be well known to you, as this is a striking disturbance of the reality function. By dint of much psychoanalytic work with these patients we established that this lack of adaptation to reality is compensated by a progressive increase in the creation of fantasies, which goes so far that the dream world becomes more real for the patient than external reality. Schreber found an excellent figurative description for this phenomenon in his delusion about the "end of the world." He thus depicts the loss of reality in a very concrete way. The dynamic explanation is simple: we say that libido has withdrawn more and more from the external world into the inner world of fantasy, and there had to create, as a substitute for the lost world, a so-called reality equivalent. This substitute is built up piece by piece, so to speak, and it is most interesting to see out of what psychological material this inner world is constructed.

273   This way of looking at the displacement of libido is based on the everyday use of the term, its original, purely sexual connotation being very rarely remembered. In actual practice we speak simply of *libido,* and this is understood in so innocuous a sense that Claparède once remarked to me that one could just as well use the word "interest." The customary use of the term has developed, quite naturally and spontaneously, into a usage which makes it possible to explain Schreber's end of the world simply as a withdrawal of libido. On this occasion Freud remembered his original sexual definition of libido and tried to come to terms with the change of meaning that had quietly taken place in the meantime. In his paper on Schreber he asks himself whether *what the psychoanalytic school calls libido and conceives as "interest from erotic sources" coincides with interest in general.* You see that, putting the problem in this way, Freud asks himself the question which Claparède had already answered in practice.

274   Freud thus broaches the question of whether the loss of reality in schizophrenia, to which I drew attention in my "Psychology of Dementia Praecox," [6] is due entirely to the withdrawal of erotic interest, or whether this coincides with objective interest in general. We can hardly suppose that the normal "fonction du réel" (Janet) is maintained solely by erotic interest. The fact

[6] [The first paper in *The Psychogenesis of Mental Disease,* Collected Works, Vol. 3.]

is that in very many cases reality disappears altogether, so that not a trace of psychological adaptation can be found in these patients. (In these states reality is replaced by complex contents.) We are therefore compelled to admit that not only the erotic interest, but all interest whatsoever, has got lost, and with it the whole adaptation to reality.

275   Earlier, in my "Psychology of Dementia Praecox," I tried to get round this difficulty by using the expression "psychic energy," because I could not base the theory of dementia praecox on the theory of displacements of libido sexually defined. My experience—at that time chiefly psychiatric—did not permit me to understand this latter theory: only later did I come to realize its partial correctness as regards the neuroses, thanks to increased experiences in the field of hysteria and obsessional neurosis. Abnormal displacements of libido, quite definitely sexual, do in fact play a great role in these illnesses. But although very characteristic repressions of sexual libido do take place in the neuroses, the loss of reality so typical of dementia praecox never occurs. In dementia praecox the loss of the reality function is so extreme that it must involve the loss of other instinctual forces whose sexual character must be denied absolutely, for no one is likely to maintain that reality is a function of sex. Moreover, if it were, the withdrawal of erotic interest in the neuroses would necessarily entail a loss of reality comparable to that which occurs in dementia praecox. But, as I said before, this is not the case.

276   ⟨Another thing to be considered—as Freud also pointed out in his work on the Schreber case—is that the introversion of sexual libido leads to an investment of the ego which might conceivably produce that effect of loss of reality. It is indeed tempting to explain the psychology of the loss in this way. But when we examine more closely the various things that can arise from the withdrawal and introversion of sexual libido, we come to see that though it can produce the psychology of an ascetic anchorite, it cannot produce dementia praecox. The anchorite's whole endeavour is to exterminate every trace of sexual interest, and this is something that cannot be asserted of dementia praecox.[7]⟩

7 (It might be objected that dementia praecox is characterized not only by the introversion of sexual libido but also by a regression to the infantile level, and

277   These facts have made it impossible for me to apply Freud's libido theory to dementia praecox. I am also of the opinion that Abraham's essay on this subject [8] is theoretically untenable from the standpoint of Freud's conception of libido. Abraham's belief that the paranoid system, or the schizophrenic symptomatology, is produced by the withdrawal of sexual libido from the outside world cannot be justified in terms of our present knowledge. For, as Freud has clearly shown, a mere introversion or regression of libido invariably leads to a neurosis and not to dementia praecox. It seems to me impossible simply to transfer the libido theory to dementia praecox, because this disease shows a loss of reality which cannot be explained solely by the loss of erotic interest.

THE GENETIC CONCEPTION OF LIBIDO

278   The attitude of reserve which I adopted towards the ubiquity of sexuality in my foreword to "The Psychology of Dementia Praecox," despite the fact that I recognized the psychological mechanisms pointed out by Freud, was dictated by the position of the libido theory at that time. Its sexual definition did not permit me to explain functional disturbances which affect the indefinite sphere of the hunger drive just as much as that of sex solely in the light of a sexual libido theory. Freud's libido theory had long seemed to me inapplicable to dementia praecox. In my analytical work I noticed that, with growing experience, a slow change in my conception of libido had taken place. Instead of the descriptive definition set forth in Freud's *Three Essays*, there gradually took shape a genetic definition of libido, which enabled me to replace the expression "psychic energy" by "libido." I had to tell myself: if the reality function consists nowadays to only a very small extent of sexual libido

that this constitutes the difference between the anchorite and the schizophrenic. This is certainly correct, but it would still have to be proved that in dementia praecox it is regularly and exclusively the erotic interest which goes into a regression. It seems to me rather difficult to prove this, because erotic interest would then have to be understood as the "Eros" of the old philosophers. But that can hardly be meant. I know cases of dementia praecox where all regard for self-preservation disappears, but not the very lively erotic interests.)

8 ["The Psycho-Sexual Differences between Hysteria and Dementia Praecox."]

and to a far greater extent of other instinctual forces, then it is very important to consider whether, phylogenetically speaking, the reality function is not, at least very largely, of sexual origin. It is impossible to answer this question directly, but we can seek to approach it by a circuitous route.

279   A cursory glance at the history of evolution suffices to show that numerous complicated functions, which today must be denied all trace of sexuality, were originally nothing but offshoots of the reproductive instinct. As we know, an important change occurred in the principles of reproduction during the ascent through the animal kingdom: the vast numbers of gametes which chance fertilization made necessary were progressively reduced in favour of assured fertilization and effective protection of the young. The decreased production of ova and spermatozoa set free considerable quantities of energy for conversion into the mechanisms of attraction and protection of offspring, etc. Thus we find the first stirrings of the artistic impulse in animals, but subservient to the reproductive instinct and limited to the breeding season. The original sexual character of these biological phenomena gradually disappears as they become organically fixed and achieve functional independence. Although there can be no doubt that music originally belonged to the reproductive sphere, it would be an unjustified and fantastic generalization to put music in the same category as sex. Such a terminology would be tantamount to treating of Cologne cathedral in a text-book of mineralogy, on the ground that it consisted very largely of stones.

280   Up to now we have spoken of libido as the instinct for propagation or for the preservation of the species, and have kept within the confines of a view which contrasts libido with hunger in the same way as the instinct for the preservation of the species is contrasted with the instinct for self-preservation. In nature, of course, this artificial distinction does not exist. There we see only a continuous life-urge, a will to live, which seeks to ensure the continuance of the whole species through the preservation of the individual. Thus far our conception of libido coincides with Schopenhauer's Will, inasmuch as a movement perceived from the outside can only be grasped as the manifestation of an inner will or desire. Once we have arrived at the bold conjecture that the libido which was originally employed in the

41

production of ova and spermatozoa is now firmly organized in the function of nest-building, for instance, and can no longer be employed otherwise, we are compelled to include every striving and every desire, as well as hunger, in this conception. There is no longer any justification for differentiating in principle between the desire to build nests and the desire to eat.[9]

281   I think you will already see where our argument is leading us. We are in the process of carrying through the energic point of view consistently, putting the energic mode of action in the place of the purely formal functioning. Just as the older sciences were always talking of reciprocal actions in nature, and this old-fashioned point of view was replaced by the law of the conservation of energy, so here too, in the realm of psychology, we are seeking to replace the reciprocal action of co-ordinated psychic faculties by an energy conceived to be homogeneous. We thus take cognizance of the justified criticism that the psychoanalytic school is operating with a mystical conception of libido.

282   For this reason I must dispel the illusion that the whole psychoanalytic school has a clearly understood and concrete conception of libido. I maintain that the libido with which we operate is not only not concrete or known, but is a complete X, a pure hypothesis, a model or counter, and is no more concretely conceivable than the energy known to the world of physics. Only in this way can we escape those violent transgressions of the proper boundaries, which happen time and again when we try to reduce co-ordinated forces to one another. (We shall never be able to explain the mechanics of solid bodies or of electromagnetic phenomena in terms of a theory of light, for mechanics and electromagnetism are not light. Moreover, strictly speaking, it is not physical forces that change into one another, but the energy that changes its outward form. Forces are phenomenal manifestations; what underlies their relations with one another is the hypothetical idea of energy, which is, of course, entirely psychological and has nothing to do with so-called objective reality.) This same conceptual achievement that has taken place in physics we seek to accomplish for the libido theory. We want to give the concept of libido the position that really belongs to it, which is a purely energic one, so that we can conceive the

9 [Pars. 278–80 and 274–75 reappear with certain modifications and additions in *Symbols of Transformation*, pars. 192ff.—EDITORS.]

life-process in terms of energy and replace the old idea of reciprocal action by relations of absolute equivalence. We shall not
be disturbed if we are met with the cry of vitalism. We are as
far removed from any belief in a specific life-force as from any
other metaphysical assertion. Libido is intended simply as a
name for the energy which manifests itself in the life-process and
is perceived subjectively as conation and desire. It is hardly necessary to defend this view. It brings us into line with a powerful
current of ideas that seeks to comprehend the world of appearances energically. Suffice it to say that everything we perceive
can only be understood as an effect of force.

283   In the diversity of natural phenomena we see desire—libido
—taking the most variegated forms. In early childhood it appears
at first wholly in the form of the nutritive instinct which builds
up the body. As the body develops, new spheres of activity are
opened up successively for the libido. A definitive and extremely
important sphere of activity is sexuality, which to begin with
appears closely bound up with the function of nutrition (one
has only to think of the influence of nutritional factors on propagation in the lower animals and plants). In the sphere of sexuality the libido acquires a form whose tremendous importance
gives us the justification for using the ambiguous term "libido"
at all. Here it appears at first in the form of an undifferentiated,
primary libido, as the energy of growth that causes cell-division,
budding, etc. in individuals.

284   Out of this primary, sexual libido, which produces from one
small organism millions of ova and spermatozoa, there developed, by a tremendous restriction of fertility, offshoots whose
function is maintained by a specifically differentiated libido.
This differentiated libido is now "desexualized" by being di-
vested of its original function of producing eggs and sperm, nor
is there any possibility of restoring it to its original function.
Thus the whole process of development consists in a progressive
absorption of the primary libido, which produced nothing but
gametes, into the secondary functions of attraction and protection of offspring. This development presupposes a quite different and much more complicated relation to reality, a genuine
reality function which is inseparably connected with the needs
of reproduction. In other words, the altered mode of reproduction brings with it, as a correlate, a correspondingly enhanced

43

adaptation to reality. This, of course, does not imply that the reality function owes its existence exclusively to the differentiation in reproduction. I am fully aware of the indefinitely large role played by the nutritive function.

285   In this way we gain some insight into the factors originally conditioning the reality function. It would be a fundamental error to say that its driving force is a sexual one. It *was* in large measure a sexual one originally, but even then not exclusively so.

286   The process of absorption of primary libido into secondary functions probably always occurred in the form of "libidinal affluxes," that is to say sexuality was diverted from its original destination and part of it used for the mechanisms of attraction and protection of the young—functions which gradually increase the higher you go in the phylogenetic scale. This transfer of sexual libido from the sexual sphere to subsidiary functions is still taking place. (Malthusianism, for instance, is an artificial continuation of the natural tendency.) Wherever this operation occurs without detriment to the adaptation of the individual we call it "sublimation," and "repression" when the attempt fails.

287   The descriptive standpoint of psychoanalysis views the multiplicity of instincts, among them the sexual instinct, as partial phenomena, and, in addition, recognizes certain affluxes of libido to nonsexual instincts.

288   The genetic standpoint is different. It regards the multiplicity of instincts as issuing from a relative unity, the libido; it sees how portions of libido continually split off from the reproductive function, add themselves as libidinal affluxes to the newly formed functions, and finally merge into them.

289   From this point of view we can rightly say that the schizophrenic withdraws his libido from the outside world and in consequence suffers a loss of reality compensated by an increase in fantasy activity.

INFANTILE PERVERSIONS

290   We shall now try to fit this new conception of libido into the theory of infantile sexuality, which is so very important for the

44

theory of neurosis. In infants we find that libido as energy, as a vital activity, first manifests itself in the nutritional zone, where, in the act of sucking, food is taken in with a rhythmic movement and with every sign of satisfaction. With the growth of the individual and development of his organs the libido creates for itself new avenues of activity. The primary model of rhythmic movement, producing pleasure and satisfaction, is now transferred to the zone of the other functions, with sexuality as its ultimate goal. A considerable portion of the "alimentary libido" has to convert itself into "sexual libido." This transition does not take place quite suddenly at puberty, but only very gradually during the course of childhood. The libido can free itself only with difficulty and quite slowly from the modality of the nutritive function in order to pass over into the sexual function.

291   In this transitional stage there are, so far as I am able to judge, two distinct phases: the phase of sucking, and the phase of displaced rhythmic activity. Sucking belongs by its very nature to the sphere of the nutritive function, but outgrows it by ceasing to be a function of nutrition and becoming a rhythmic activity aiming at pleasure and satisfaction without intake of nourishment. At this point the hand comes in as an auxiliary organ. It appears even more clearly as an auxiliary organ in the phase of displaced rhythmic activity for pleasure, which then leaves the oral zone and turns to other regions. As a rule, it is the other body-openings that become the first objects of libidinal interest; then the skin, or special parts of it. The activities carried out in these places, taking the form of rubbing, boring, picking, pulling, and so forth, follow a certain rhythm and serve to produce pleasure. After lingering for a while at these stations, the libido continues its wanderings until it reaches the sexual zone, where it may provide occasion for the first attempts at masturbation. In the course of its migrations the libido carries traces of the nutritional phase into its new field of operations, which readily accounts for the many intimate connections between the nutritive and the sexual function.[10] This migration of libido takes place during the presexual stage, whose special distinguishing-mark is that the libido gradually sloughs off the

10 [Pars. 290–91 likewise recur with small changes in *Symbols of Transformation*, par. 206.—EDITORS.]

character of the nutritive instinct and assumes that of the sexual instinct.[11] At the stage of nutrition, therefore, we cannot yet speak of a true sexual libido.

292   In consequence, we are obliged to qualify the so-called polymorphous-perverse sexuality of early infancy. The polymorphism of libidinal strivings at this period can be explained as the gradual migration of libido, stage by stage, away from the sphere of the nutritive function into that of the sexual function. Thus the term "perverse," so bitterly attacked by our critics, can be dropped, since it creates a false impression.

293   When a chemical substance breaks up into its elements, these elements are, under those conditions, products of disintegration. But it is not permissible to describe all elements whatsoever as products of disintegration. Perversions are disturbed products of a developed sexuality. They are never the initial stages of sexuality, although there is an undoubted similarity between the initial stage and the product of disintegration. As sexuality develops, its infantile stages, which should no longer be regarded as "perverse" but as rudimentary and provisional, resolve themselves into normal sexuality. The more smoothly the libido withdraws from its provisional positions, the more quickly · and completely does the formation of normal sexuality take place. It is of the essence of normal sexuality that all those early infantile tendencies which are not yet sexual should be sloughed off as much as possible. The less this is so, the more perverse will sexuality become. Here the expression "perverse" is altogether appropriate. The basic conditioning factor in perversion, therefore, is an infantile, insufficiently developed state of sexuality. The expression "polymorphous-perverse" has been borrowed from the psychology of neurosis and projected backwards into the psychology of the child, where of course it is quite out of place.

11 ⟨I must ask the reader not to misunderstand my figurative way of speaking. It is, of course, not libido as energy that gradually frees itself from the function of nutrition, but libido as a function, which is bound up with the slow changes of organic growth.⟩

4. NEUROSIS AND AETIOLOGICAL FACTORS
IN CHILDHOOD

294   Now that we have ascertained what is to be understood by
infantile sexuality, we can follow up the discussion of the theory
of neurosis, which we began in the first lecture and then
dropped. We followed the theory of neurosis up to the point
where we ran up against Freud's statement that the predisposition which makes traumatic experiences pathogenically effective is a sexual one. Helped by our reflections since then, we
can now understand how that sexual predisposition is to be conceived: it is a retardation, a check in the process of freeing the
libido from the activities of the presexual stage. The disturbance must be regarded in the first place as a temporary fixation:
the libido lingers too long at certain stations in the course of its
migration from the nutritive function to the sexual function.
This produces a state of disharmony because provisional and,
as it were, outworn activities still persist at a period when they
should have been given up. This formula can be applied to all
those infantile features which are so prevalent in neurotics that
no attentive observer can have failed to notice them. In dementia praecox the infantilism is so striking that it has even
given a telltale name to one particular syndrome—*hebephrenia*
(literally, 'adolescent mind').

295   The matter is not ended, however, by saying that the libido
lingers too long in the preliminary stages. For while the libido
is lingering, time does not stand still, and the development of
the individual is proceeding apace. Physical maturation heightens the discrepancy between the perseverating infantile activity
and the demands of later years with their changed conditions
of life. In this way the foundation is laid for a dissociation of the
personality, and hence for a conflict, which is the real basis of a
neurosis. The more the libido is engaged in retarded activities,
the more intense will the conflict be. The particular experience

47

best suited to make this conflict manifest is a traumatic or pathogenic one.

296   As Freud has shown in his early writings, one can easily
imagine a neurosis arising in this way. It was a conception that
fitted in quite well with the views of Janet, who attributed a
neurosis to some kind of defect. From this standpoint one could
regard neurosis as a product of retarded affective development,
and I can easily imagine that this conception must seem self-
evident to anyone who is inclined to derive the neuroses more
or less directly from a hereditary taint or congenital degeneracy.
Unfortunately the real state of affairs is much more complicated. In order to give you some idea of these complications, I
shall cite a very ordinary example of hysteria, which I hope will
show you how characteristic and how extremely important they
are theoretically.

297   You will probably remember the case of the young hysteric
I mentioned earlier, who, surprisingly enough, did not react to
a situation which might have been expected to make a profound
impression on her, and yet displayed an unexpected and patho-
logically violent reaction to a quite ordinary occurrence. We
took this occasion to express our doubt as to the aetiological
significance of the trauma, and to investigate more closely the
so-called predisposition which rendered the trauma effective.
The result of that investigation led to the conclusion just mentioned, that it is by no means improbable that the origin of a
neurosis is due to a retardation of affective development.

298   You will now ask in what way the patient's affective development was retarded. The answer is that she lived in a world of
fantasy which can only be described as infantile. It is unnecessary for me to give you a description of these fantasies, for, as
neurologists or psychiatrists, you undoubtedly have a daily opportunity to listen to the childish prejudices, illusions, and emotional demands of neurotics. The disinclination to face stern
reality is the distinguishing feature of these fantasies; there is a
lack of seriousness, a playfulness in them, which sometimes
frivolously disguises real difficulties, at other times makes mountains out of molehills, always thinking up fantastic ways of
evading the demands of real life. We immediately recognize in
them the intemperate psychic attitude of the child to reality, his
precarious judgment, his lack of orientation, his dislike of un-

pleasant duties. With such an infantile mentality all manner of wishful fantasies and illusions can grow luxuriantly, and this is where the danger comes in. By means of these fantasies people can easily slip into an unreal and completely unadapted attitude to the world, which sooner or later must lead to catastrophe.

THE TRAUMA THEORY CRITICIZED

299   If we follow the patient's infantile fantasy-life back into earliest childhood, we find, it is true, many obviously outstanding scenes which might well serve to provide fresh food for this or that fantastic variation, but it would be vain to search for the so-called traumatic elements from which something pathological, for instance her abnormal fantasy activity, might have originated. There were plenty of "traumatic" scenes, but they did not lie in early childhood; and the few scenes of early childhood which were remembered did not appear to be traumatic, being more like accidental experiences which passed by without having any effect worth mentioning on her fantasies. The earliest fantasies consisted of all sorts of vague and half-understood impressions she had received of her parents. All sorts of special feelings clustered round the father, fluctuating between fear, horror, aversion, disgust, love, and ecstasy. The case was like so many other cases of hysteria for which no traumatic aetiology can be found; they are rooted instead in a peculiar, premature fantasy activity which permanently retains its infantile character.

300   You will object that it is just that scene with the bolting horses that represents the trauma, and that this was obviously the model for that nocturnal scene eighteen years later, when the patient could not get out of the way of the horses trotting along behind her and wanted to throw herself into the river, following the model of the horses and carriage plunging down the ravine. From this moment on she also suffered from hysterical twilight states. But, as I tried to show you in my earlier lecture, we find no trace of any such aetiological connection in the development of her fantasy system. It is as though the danger of losing her life, that first time with the bolting horses, passed by without noticeable effect. In all the years following

49

that experience there was no discernible trace of that fright. It was as though it had never happened. In parenthesis let me add that perhaps it never happened at all. There is nothing to prevent it from being sheer fantasy, for here I have only the statements of the patient to rely on.[1]

301   Suddenly, after eighteen years, this experience becomes significant, is reproduced and acted out in all its details. The old theory says: the previously blocked affect has suddenly forced its way to the surface. This assumption is extremely unlikely and becomes still more inconceivable when we consider that the story of the bolting horses may not even be true. Be that as it may, it is almost inconceivable that an affect should remain buried for years and then suddenly explode at an unsuitable opportunity.

302   It is very suspicious, too, that patients often have a pronounced tendency to account for their ailments by some long-past experience, ingeniously drawing the analyst's attention away from the present to some false track in the past. This false track was the one pursued by the first psychoanalytical theory. But to this false hypothesis we owe an insight into the determination of neurotic symptoms which we should never have reached if the investigators had not trodden this path, guided into it, really, by the tendency of the patient to mislead. I think that only those who regard the happenings in this world as a concatenation of errors and accidents, and who therefore believe that the pedagogic hand of the rationalist is constantly needed to guide us, can ever imagine that this path was an aberration from which we should have been warned off with a signboard. Besides the deeper insight into psychological determination, we owe to this "error" a method of inquiry of incalculable importance. It is for us to rejoice and be thankful that Freud had the courage to let himself be guided along this path. Not thus is the progress of science hindered, but rather by blind adherence to insights once gained, by the typical conservatism of authority, by the childish vanity of the savant and his fear of making mistakes. This lack of courage is considerably more injurious to the name of science than an honest error. When

1 (It may not be superfluous to remark that there are still people who believe that psychologists swallow the lies of their patients. That is quite impossible. Lies are fantasies, and we deal in fantasies.)

will there be an end to the incessant squabbling about who is right? One has only to look at the history of science: how many have *been* right, and how few have *remained* right!

THE PARENTAL COMPLEX

303   But to return to our case. The question that now arises is this: if the old trauma is not of aetiological significance, then the cause of the manifest neurosis is obviously to be sought in the retardation of affective development. We must therefore regard the patient's statement that her hysterical twilight states were caused by the fright she got with the horses as null and void, although that fright was the starting-point for her manifest illness. This experience merely *seems* to be important without being so in reality, a formulation which is true of most other traumata. They merely *seem* to be important because they provide occasion for the manifestation of a condition that has long been abnormal. The abnormal condition, as we have already explained, consists in the anachronistic persistence of an infantile stage of libido development. The patients continue to hang on to forms of libido activity which they should have abandoned long ago. It is almost impossible to catalogue these forms, so extraordinarily varied are they. The commonest, which is scarcely ever absent, is an excessive fantasy activity characterized by a thoughtless overvaluation of subjective wishes. Excessive fantasy activity is always a sign of faulty application of libido to reality. Instead of being used for the best possible adaptation to the actual circumstances, it gets stuck in fantastic applications. We call this state one of partial introversion when libido is used for the maintenance of fantasies and illusions instead of being adapted to the actual conditions of life.

304   A regular concomitant of this retardation of affective development is the *parental complex*. When the libido is not used for purposes of real adaptation it is always more or less introverted.[2] The material content of the psychic world consists of

2 (Introversion does not mean that libido simply accumulates inactively. But it is used for the creation of fantasies and illusions when the introversion results in regression to an infantile mode of adaptation. Introversion can also lead to action on a rational plane.)

memories, that is, of material from the individual's past (aside from actual perceptions). If the libido is partially or totally introverted, it invests to a greater or lesser degree large areas of memory, with the result that these reminiscences acquire a vitality that no longer properly belongs to them. The patients then live more or less entirely in the world of the past. They battle with difficulties which once played a role in their lives but which ought to have faded out long ago. They still worry, or rather are forced to worry, about things which should long since have ceased to be important. They amuse or torment themselves with fancies which, in the normal course of events, were once significant but no longer have any significance for adults.

305   Among the things that were of the utmost significance at the infantile period the most influential are the personalities of the parents. Even when the parents have long been dead and have lost, or should have lost, all significance, the situation of the patient having perhaps completely changed since then, they are still somehow present and as important as if they were still alive. The patient's love, admiration, resistance, hatred, and rebelliousness still cling to their effigies, transfigured by affection or distorted by envy, and often bearing little resemblance to the erstwhile reality. It was this fact that compelled me to speak no longer of "father" and "mother" but to employ instead the term "imago," because these fantasies are not concerned any more with the real father and mother but with subjective and often very much distorted images of them which lead a shadowy but nonetheless potent existence in the mind of the patient.

306   The complex of the parental imagos, that is, the whole tissue of ideas relating to the parents, provides an important field of activity for the introverted libido. I should mention in passing that the complex in itself leads but a shadowy existence if it is not invested with libido. In accordance with the earlier usage worked out in my *Studies in Word Association*, the word "complex" denoted a system of ideas already invested with libido and activated by it. But this system also exists *in potentia*, ready for possible action, even when not temporarily or permanently invested with libido.

PARENTAL INFLUENCES ON CHILDREN

307 At the time when psychoanalytic theory was still dominated by the trauma concept and, in conformity with that view, was inclined to look for the *causa efficiens* of the neurosis in the past, it seemed to us that the parental complex was, as Freud called it, the "nuclear complex" of neurosis. The role of the parents seemed to be so powerful a factor that we were apt to blame them for all the subsequent complications in the life of the patient. Some years ago I discussed this in my paper, "The Significance of the Father in the Destiny of the Individual." [3] Once again we had allowed ourselves to be guided by the tendency of the patient to revert to the past, following the direction of his introverted libido. This time, certainly, it was no longer an external, accidental experience or event which seemed to produce the pathogenic effect; it was rather a psychological effect apparently arising out of the individual's difficulties in adapting to the conditions of the family milieu. The disharmony between the parents on the one hand and between the parents and the child on the other seemed especially liable to produce psychic currents in the child which were incompatible with his individual way of life.

308 In the paper just alluded to I cited a number of instances, taken from a wealth of material on this subject, which show these effects particularly clearly. The effects apparently emanating from the parents are not limited to the endless recriminations of their neurotic offspring, who constantly lay the blame for their illness on their family circumstances or bad upbringing, but extend even to actual events in the life of the patients, where no such determining influence could have been expected. The lively imitativeness which we find in primitives as well as in children can give rise, in particularly sensitive children, to a peculiar inner identification with the parents, to a mental attitude so similar to theirs that effects in real life are sometimes produced which, even in detail, resemble the personal experiences of the parents.[4]

[3] [See infra, pars. 693ff.]
[4] (I am discounting the inherited organic similarity which is naturally responsible for many things but by no means all.)

309   For the empirical material on this subject, I must refer you to the literature, but should just like to remind you that one of my pupils, Dr. Emma Fürst, has adduced valuable experimental proofs in regard to this problem. I have already referred to her researches in my lectures at Clark University.[5] By applying the association test to whole families, Dr. Fürst established the great conformity of reaction type among all members of one family. These experiments show that very often there exists an unconscious concordance of association between parents and children, which can only be explained as an intensive imitation or identification. The results of these researches indicate a far-reaching parallelism of biological tendencies that readily explains the sometimes astonishing similarity in the destinies of parents and children. Our destinies are as a rule the outcome of our psychological tendencies.

310   These facts enable us to understand why not only the patients themselves, but the theories that have been built on these researches, tend to assume that neurosis is the result of the characterological influence of the parents on the children. This assumption is, moreover, supported by the experience which lies at the base of all education, namely, the plasticity of the child's mind, which is commonly compared with soft wax, taking up and preserving all impressions. We know that the first impressions of childhood accompany us inalienably throughout life, and that, just as indestructibly, certain educational influences can keep people all their lives within those limits. In these circumstances it is not surprising that conflicts break out between the personality moulded by educational and other influences of the infantile milieu and one's own individual style of life. It is a conflict which all those must face who are called upon to live a life that is independent and creative.

311   Owing to the enormous influence which childhood has on the later development of character, you will readily understand why one would like to attribute the cause of a neurosis directly to the influences of the infantile environment. I/ must confess

5 [Fürst, "Statistical Investigations on Word-Associations and on Familial Agreement in Reaction Type among Uneducated Persons" (orig. 1905). Jung's discussion of her work occurred in the second of the Clark Lectures under the title "Familial Constellations"; see *Experimental Researches*, Coll. Works, Vol. 2.—EDITORS.]

that I have known cases in which any other explanation seemed to me less plausible. There are indeed parents whose own contradictory nature causes them to treat their children in so unreasonable a fashion that the children's illness would appear to be unavoidable. Hence it is almost a rule among nerve specialists to remove neurotic children, whenever possible, from the dangerous family atmosphere and place them among more healthy influences, where, even without any medical treatment, they thrive much better than at home. There are many neurotic patients who were clearly neurotic as children and so have never been free from illness since childhood. In such cases the view outlined above seems generally valid.

THE INFANTILE MENTALITY

312　　This knowledge, which for the time being seemed to us definitive, was considerably deepened by the researches of Freud and the psychoanalytic school. The parent-child relationship was studied in all its details, since it was just this relationship which was considered aetiologically important. It was soon noticed that these patients really did live partly or entirely in their childhood world, although themselves quite unconscious of this fact. On the contrary, it was the arduous task of psychoanalysis to investigate the psychological mode of adaptation so thoroughly that one could put one's finger on the infantile misunderstandings. As you know, a striking number of neurotics were spoiled as children. Such cases offer the best and clearest examples of the infantilism of their psychological mode of adaptation. They start out in life expecting the same friendly reception, tenderness, and easy success to which they were accustomed by their parents in their youth. Even very intelligent patients are incapable of seeing that from the very beginning they owe the complications of their lives as well as their neurosis to dragging their infantile emotional attitude along with them. The small world of the child, the family milieu, is the model for the big world. The more intensely the family sets its stamp on the child, the more he will be emotionally inclined, as an adult, to see in the great world his former small world. Of course this must not be taken as a conscious intellectual process. On the contrary, the patient feels and sees the difference between now and then, and tries as well as he can to adapt himself. Perhaps he will even believe himself perfectly adapted, since he may be able to grasp the situation intellectually, but that does not prevent his emotions from lagging far behind his intellectual insight.

313   It is scarcely necessary to give you examples of this phenomenon, for it is an everyday experience that our emotions never come up to the level of our insight. It is exactly the same with the neurotic, but greatly intensified. He may perhaps believe that, except for his neurosis, he is a normal person, fully adapted to the conditions of life. It never crosses his mind that he has still not given up certain infantile demands, that he still carries with him, in the background, expectations and illusions of which he has never made himself conscious. He indulges in all sorts of pet fantasies, of which he is seldom, if ever, so conscious that he knows that he has them. Very often they exist only as emotional expectations, hopes, prejudices, and so forth. In this case we call them unconscious fantasies. Sometimes they appear on the fringe of consciousness as fleeting thoughts, only to vanish again the next moment, so that the patient is unable to say whether he had such fantasies or not. It is only during psychoanalytic treatment that most patients learn to retain and observe these fugitive thoughts. Although most fantasies were once conscious, for a moment, as fleeting thoughts, it would not do to call them *conscious*, because most of the time they are practically *unconscious*. It is therefore right to call them unconscious fantasies. Of course there are also infantile fantasies which are perfectly conscious and can be reproduced at any time.

5. THE FANTASIES OF THE UNCONSCIOUS

314   The realm of unconscious infantile fantasies has become the real object of psychoanalytic research, for it seems to offer the key to the aetiology of neurosis. Here, quite otherwise than with the trauma theory, we are forced by all the reasons we have mentioned to assume that the roots of the psychological present are to be found in the family history of the patient.

315   The fantasy systems which patients present on being questioned are mostly of a composite nature and are elaborated like a novel or a drama. But, despite their elaboration, they are of relatively little value in investigating the unconscious. Just because they are conscious, they defer too much to the demands of etiquette and social morality. They have been purged of all painful personal details, and also of everything ugly, thereby becoming socially presentable and revealing very little. The more valuable and evidently more influential fantasies are not conscious, in the sense previously defined, and so have to be dug out by the psychoanalytic technique.

316   Without wishing to enter fully into the question of technique, I must here meet an objection that is constantly heard. It is that the so-called unconscious fantasies are merely suggested to the patient and exist only in the mind of the analyst. This objection is on the same vulgar level as those which impute to us the crude mistakes of beginners. Only people with no psychological experience and no knowledge of the history of psychology are capable of making such accusations. No one with the faintest glimmering of mythology could possibly fail to see the startling parallels between the unconscious fantasies brought to light by the psychoanalytic school and mythological ideas. The objection that our knowledge of mythology has been suggested to the patient is without foundation, because the psychoanalytic school discovered the fantasies first and only then became acquainted with their mythology. Mythology, as we know, is something quite outside the ken of the medical man.

317   As these fantasies are unconscious, the patient is naturally unaware of their existence, and to question him about them directly would be quite pointless. Nevertheless it is said over and over again, not only by patients but by so-called normal persons: "But if I had such fantasies, surely I would know it!" But what is unconscious is in truth something that we do *not* know. Our opponents, too, are firmly convinced that such things do not exist. This *a priori* judgment is pure scholasticism and has no grounds to support it. We cannot possibly rest on the dogma that consciousness alone is the psyche, for we have daily proof that our consciousness is only a part of the psychic function. When the contents of our consciousness appear they are already in a highly complex state; the constellation of our thoughts from the material contained in our memory is a predominantly unconscious process. We are therefore obliged to assume, whether we like it or not, the existence of a non-conscious psychic sphere, even if only as a "negative borderline concept," like Kant's *Ding an sich*. Since we perceive effects whose origin cannot be found in consciousness, we are compelled to allow hypothetical contents to the sphere of the non-conscious, which means presupposing that the origin of those effects lies in the unconscious precisely because it is not conscious. This conception of the unconscious can hardly be accused of "mysticism." We do not pretend to know or to assert anything positive about the state of psychic elements in the unconscious. Instead, we have formulated symbolical concepts in a manner analogous to our formulation of conscious concepts, and this terminology has proved its value in practice.

THE CONCEPT OF THE UNCONSCIOUS

318   This way of thinking is the only possible one if we accept the axiom that "principles are not to be multiplied beyond the necessary." We therefore speak about the effects of the unconscious just as we do about the phenomena of consciousness. Great objection was taken to Freud's statement: "The unconscious can only wish." This was regarded as an unheard-of metaphysical assertion, something like a tenet from von Hartmann's *Philosophy of the Unconscious*. The indignation was

due simply to the fact that these critics, unknown to themselves, evidently started from a metaphysical conception of the unconscious as an *ens per se,* and naïvely projected their epistemologically unclarified ideas on to us. For us the unconscious is not an entity in this sense but a mere term, about whose metaphysical essence we do not permit ourselves to form any idea. In this we are unlike those arm-chair psychologists who are not only perfectly informed about the localization of the psyche in the brain and the physiological correlates of mental processes, but can assert positively that beyond consciousness there are nothing but "physiological processes in the cortex."

319   Such naïvetés should not be imputed to us. When Freud says that the unconscious can only wish, he is describing in symbolical terms effects whose source is not conscious, but which from the standpoint of conscious thinking can only be regarded as analogous to wishes. The psychoanalytic school is, moreover, aware that the discussion as to whether "wishing" is a suitable analogy or not can be reopened at any time. Anybody who knows a better one will be welcome. Instead of which, our opponents content themselves with denying the existence of these phenomena or else, if certain phenomena have to be admitted, they abstain from all theoretical formulations. This last point is understandable enough, since it is not everyone's business to think theoretically.

320   Once one has succeeded in freeing oneself from the dogma of the psyche's identity with consciousness, thus admitting the possible existence of extra-conscious psychic processes, one cannot, *a priori,* either assert or deny anything about the potentialities of the unconscious. The psychoanalytic school has been accused of making assertions without sufficient grounds. It seems to us that the abundant, perhaps too abundant case-material contained in the literature offers enough and more than enough grounds, yet it does not seem sufficient for our opponents. There must be a good deal of difference as to the meaning of the word "sufficient" in regard to the validity of these grounds. So we must ask: Why does the psychoanalytic school apparently demand far less exacting proofs of its formulations than its opponents?

321   The reason is simple. An engineer who has built a bridge and calculated its load needs no further proof of its holding

capacity. But a sceptical layman, who has no notion how a bridge is built, or what is the strength of the material used, will demand quite different proofs of its holding capacity, since he can have no confidence in it. It is chiefly the profound ignorance of our opponents about what we are doing that screws their demands up to such a pitch. In the second place, there are the countless theoretical misunderstandings: it is impossible for us to know them all and to clear them up. Just as we find in our patients new and ever more astounding misconceptions about the ways and aims of psychoanalysis, so our critics display an inexhaustible ingenuity in misunderstanding. You can see from our discussion of the concept of the unconscious just what kind of false philosophical assumptions can vitiate understanding of our terminology. Obviously a person who thinks of the unconscious as an absolute entity is bound to require proofs of a totally different kind, utterly beyond our power to give, as our opponents in fact do. Had we to offer proof of immortality, mountains of proofs of the weightiest nature would have to be furnished, very different from what would be required to demonstrate the existence of plasmodia in a malaria patient. Metaphysical expectations still bedevil scientific thinking far too much for the problems of psychoanalysis to be seen in their own frame of reference.

322   But, in fairness to our critics, I must admit that the psychoanalytic school has itself given rise to plenty of misunderstandings, even though in all innocence. One of the principal sources is the confusion that reigns in the theoretical sphere. Regrettable though it is, we have no presentable theory. You would understand this if you could see in concrete instances the enormous difficulties we have to wrestle with. Contrary to the opinion of nearly all the critics, Freud is anything rather than a theorist. He is an empiricist, as anyone must admit who is willing to go at all deeply into Freud's writings and to try to see his cases as he sees them. Unfortunately, our critics are not willing. As we have repeatedly been told, it is "repulsive and disgusting" to see them as Freud does. But how can anyone learn the nature of Freud's method if he allows himself to be put off by disgust? Just because people make no effort to accommodate themselves to Freud's point of view, adopted perhaps as a necessary working hypothesis, they come to the absurd conclusion

that he is a theorist. They readily assume that *Three Essays on the Theory of Sexuality* is simply a theory, invented by a speculative brain, and that everything is put into the patient's head by suggestion. But that is turning things upside down. This makes it easy for the critics, which is just what they want. They pay no attention at all to the "couple of case-histories" with which the psychoanalyst conscientiously documents his theoretical statements, but only to the theory and the formulation of technique. The weak spots of psychoanalysis are not to be found here—for psychoanalysis is essentially empirical—though here, undoubtedly, is a large and insufficiently cultivated field where the critics can romp to their heart's content. In the field of theory there are many uncertainties and not a few contradictions. We were conscious of this long before our learned critics began to honour us with their attentions.

THE DREAM

323   After this digression we will return to the question of unconscious fantasies which occupied us before. Nobody, as we have seen, has the right to assert their existence or define their qualities unless effects of unconscious origin are observed which can be expressed in terms of conscious symbolism. The only question is whether effects can in fact be found that comply with this expectation. The psychoanalytic school believes it has discovered such effects. I will mention the principal phenomenon at once: the dream.

324   Of this it may be said that it enters consciousness as a complex structure compounded of elements whose connection with each other is not conscious. Only afterwards, by adding a series of associations to the individual images in the dream, can we show that these images had their origin in certain memories of the recent past. We ask ourselves: Where have I seen or heard that? And then, by the ordinary process of association, comes the memory that certain parts of the dream have been consciously experienced, some the day before, some earlier. So far there will be general agreement, for these things have been known for a long time. To that extent the dream presents itself to us as a more or less unintelligible jumble of elements not at

first conscious and only recognized afterwards through their associations.[1] It should be added that not all parts of the dream have a recognizable quality from which their conscious character can be deduced; they are often, and indeed mostly, unrecognizable at first. Only afterwards does it occur to us that we have consciously experienced this or that part of the dream. From this standpoint alone we may regard the dream as a product of unconscious origin.

325   The technique for exploring the unconscious origin is the one I have just mentioned, used as a matter of course long before Freud by every dream-investigator. We simply try to remember where the parts of the dream came from. The psychoanalytic technique of dream elucidation is based on this very simple principle. It is a fact that certain parts of the dream are derived from our waking life, from events which, on account of their obvious unimportance, would have fallen into oblivion and were already on the way to becoming definitely unconscious. It is just these parts that are the effects of "unconscious ideas." Exception has been taken to this expression too. Naturally we do not take things nearly so concretely, not to say ponderously, as our critics. Certainly this expression is nothing more than conscious symbolism—we were never in any doubt on that point. But it is perfectly clear and serves very well as a sign for an unknown psychic fact. As I have said before, we have no alternative but to conceive the unconscious by analogy with the conscious. We do not pretend that we understand a thing merely because we have invented a sonorous and all-but-incomprehensible name for it.

THE METHOD OF DREAM-ANALYSIS

326   The principle of psychoanalytic elucidation is, therefore, extraordinarily simple and has actually been known for a long time. The subsequent procedure follows logically along the

1 (This might be disputed on the ground that it is an *a priori* assertion. I must remark, however, that this view conforms to the one generally accepted working hypothesis concerning the origin of dreams: that they are derived from the experiences and thoughts of the recent past. We are, therefore, moving on known ground.)

same lines. If we get really absorbed in a dream—which naturally never happens outside analysis—we shall succeed in discovering still more reminiscences about the individual dream-parts. But we are not always successful in finding reminiscences about some of them. These must be put aside for the time being. ⟨When I say "reminiscences" I do not mean only memories of actual experiences; I also mean the reproduction of meaningful associations and connections.⟩ The reminiscences so gathered are called the "dream-material." We treat this material in accordance with a generally accepted scientific principle. If you have any experimental material to work up, you compare its individual parts and classify them according to their similarities. You proceed in exactly the same way with dream-material; you look for the common features, whether of form or content.

327 In doing this one has to get rid, so far as possible, of certain prejudices. I have observed that the beginner is always looking for some special feature and then tries to force his material to conform to his expectations. I have noticed this particularly with colleagues who, because of the well-known prejudices and misunderstandings, were once passionate opponents of psychoanalysis. If it was my fate to analyse them, and they at last obtained real insight into the method, the first mistake they generally made in their psychoanalytic work was to do violence to the material by their own preconceived opinions. That is, they now vented their previous attitude to psychoanalysis on their material, which they could not assess objectively but only in terms of their subjective fantasies.

328 Once embarked on the task of examining the dream-material, you must not shrink from any comparison. The material usually consists of very disparate images, from which it is sometimes very difficult to extract the *tertium comparationis*. I must refrain from giving detailed·examples, as it is quite impossible to discuss such voluminous material in a lecture. I would, however, like to call your attention to a paper by Rank on "a dream which interprets itself." [2] There you will see how extensive is the material that must be taken into account for purposes of comparison.

329 Hence, in exploring the unconscious, we proceed in the

[2] "Ein Traum, der sich selbst deutet" (1910).

usual way when conclusions are to be drawn by the comparative method. It has often been objected: Why should a dream have any unconscious content at all? This objection is in my view about as unscientific as it could possibly be. Every psychological element has its special history. Every sentence I utter has, besides the meaning consciously intended by me, its historical meaning, which may turn out to be quite different from its conscious meaning. I am expressing myself somewhat paradoxically on purpose: I do not mean that I could explain the historical meaning of every individual sentence. That is easier in the case of larger and more complex structures. Thus, it will be clear to everyone that, apart from the manifest content of a poem, the poem itself is especially characteristic of the poet in regard to its form, content, and manner of origin. While the poet merely gave expression in his poem to the mood of the moment, the literary historian will see things in it and behind it which the poet would never have suspected. The analysis which the literary historian makes of the poet's material is exactly comparable with the method of psychoanalysis, not excluding the mistakes that may creep in.

330 The psychoanalytic method can be compared with historical analysis and synthesis in general. Suppose, for instance, we did not understand the meaning of the baptismal rite practised in our churches today. The priest tells us: baptism means the admission of the child into the Christian community. But this does not satisfy us. Why is the child sprinkled with water? In order to understand this ceremony, we must gather together from the whole history of ritual, that is, from mankind's memories of the relevant traditions, a body of comparative material culled from the most varied sources:

1. Baptism is clearly a rite of initiation, a consecration. Therefore we have to collect all memories in which any initiation rites are preserved.

2. The act of baptism is performed with water. For this special form another series of memories must be collected, namely, of rites in which water is used.

3. The person to be baptized is sprinkled with water. Here we have to collect all those rites in which the neophyte is sprinkled, immersed, etc.

4. All reminiscences from mythology, folklore, as well as

superstitious practices, etc., have to be recalled, in so far as they run in any way parallel to the symbolism of the baptismal act.

331   In this way we build up a comparative study of the act of baptism. We discover the elements out of which the baptismal act is formed; we ascertain, further, its original meaning, and at the same time become acquainted with the rich world of myths that have laid the foundation of religions and help us to understand the manifold and profound meanings of baptism. The analyst proceeds in the same way with a dream. He collects the historical parallels to every part of the dream, even the remotest, and tries to reconstruct the psychological history of the dream and its underlying meanings. Through this monographic elaboration we obtain, just as in the analysis of baptism, a profound insight into the marvellously delicate and meaningful network of unconscious determination—an insight that may legitimately be compared with the historical understanding of an act which we had hitherto regarded in a very superficial and one-sided way.

332   This excursus seemed to me unavoidable. In view of the numerous misunderstandings of all those who constantly seek to discredit the psychoanalytic method, I felt obliged to give you a very general account of the method and its position within the methodology of science. I do not doubt that there are superficial and improper applications of this method. But an intelligent critic should not allow this to detract from the method itself, any more than a bad surgeon should be used to discredit the value of surgery in general. I do not doubt, either, that not all the expositions of dream-psychology by psychoanalysts are entirely free from misunderstandings and distortions. But much of this is due to the fact that, precisely because of his training in the natural sciences, it is difficult for the medical man to get an intellectual grasp of a very subtle psychological method, even though he instinctively handles it correctly.

333   The method I have described is the one I adopt and the one to which I hold myself scientifically responsible. To give advice about dreams and to make direct attempts at interpretation is, in my opinion, absolutely wrong and scientifically inadmissible. It is not a methodological but a quite arbitrary proceeding which defeats itself by the sterility of its results, like every false method.

334   If I have made the attempt to illustrate the principles of the psychoanalytic method by means of dream-analysis it is because the dream is one of the clearest examples of psychic contents whose composition eludes direct understanding. When someone knocks in a nail with a hammer in order to hang something up, we can understand every detail of the action; it is immediately evident. It is otherwise with the act of baptism, where every phase is problematic. We call these actions, whose meaning and purpose are not immediately evident, symbolic actions, or symbols. On the basis of this reasoning we call a dream symbolic, because it is a psychological product whose origin, meaning, and purpose are obscure, and.is therefore one of the purest products of unconscious constellation. As Freud aptly says, the dream is the *via regia* to the unconscious.

THE ASSOCIATION EXPERIMENT

335   There are many products of unconscious constellation besides dreams. In the association experiment we have a means of determining exactly the influence of the unconscious. We see these effects in the disturbances which I have called "complex indicators." The task which the association test sets the subject of the experiment is so extraordinarily simple that even children can accomplish it without difficulty. It is all the more surprising that, despite this, so many disturbances of the intended action should be registered. The only things that can regularly be shown to be causes of these disturbances are the partly conscious, partly unconscious constellations caused by complexes. In the majority of cases the connection of these disturbances with feeling-toned complexes can be demonstrated without difficulty. But very often we must have recourse to the psychoanalytic method in order to explain the connection; that is, we must ask the patient what associations he can give to the disturbed reactions.

336   In this way we obtain the historical material on which to base our judgment. It has been objected that the patient could then say whatever he liked—in other words, any old nonsense. This objection is made, I believe, on the unconscious assumption that the historian who gathers material for his monograph

is an imbecile, incapable of distinguishing real parallels from apparent ones and authentic reports from crude falsifications. The professional has means at his disposal for avoiding clumsy mistakes with certainty and more subtle ones with some probability. For anyone who understands psychoanalytic work it is a well-known fact that it is not so very difficult to see where there is coherence and where there is none. In addition, fraudulent statements are in the first place very significant of the person who makes them, and secondly they are easily recognized as fraudulent.

337 ⟨There is, however, another objection to be considered, which is more worth mentioning. One can ask oneself whether the reminiscences subsequently produced were really the basis of a dream. If, in the evening, I read an interesting account of a battle, and at night dream of the Balkan War, and then during analysis remember by association certain details in the account of the battle, even the most rigorous critic will fairly assume that my retrospective association is right and true. As I mentioned earlier, this is one of the most firmly entrenched hypotheses regarding the origin of dreams. All we have done is to apply this working hypothesis consistently to all the remaining associations relating to all other parts of the dream. Ultimately, we are saying no more than that this dream-element is linked with this association, that it therefore has something to do with it, that there is a connection between the two things. When a distinguished critic once remarked that, by means of psychoanalytic interpretations, one could even connect a cucumber with an elephant, this worthy showed us, by the very fact of associating "cucumber" with "elephant," that these two things somehow have an associative connection in his mind. One must have a lot of nerve and a magisterial judgment to declare that the human mind produces entirely meaningless associations. In this instance, only a little reflection is needed to understand the meaning of the association.⟩

338 In the association experiment we can ascertain the extraordinarily intense effects emanating from the unconscious precisely through the interference of complexes. The slips and faults in the experiment are nothing but prototypes of the mistakes we make in everyday life, the majority of which must be regarded as due to the interference of complexes. Freud has gathered

67

this material together in his book *The Psychopathology of Everyday Life*. It includes the so-called symptomatic actions—which from another point of view might equally well be called "symbolic actions"—and real slips like lapses of memory, slips of the tongue, and so on. All these phenomena are effects of unconscious constellations and are therefore so many gateways to the realm of the unconscious. When they are cumulative, we have to call them a neurosis, which from this point of view looks like a dysfunction and must be understood as the effect of an unconscious constellation.

339   Thus the association experiment is, not infrequently, a means of unlocking the unconscious directly, although mostly it is simply a technique for obtaining a wide selection of faulty reactions which can then be used for exploring the unconscious by psychoanalysis. At least, this is its most reliable form of application at present. However, it is possible that it will furnish other, especially valuable facts which would give us direct glimpses of the unconscious, but I do not consider this question sufficiently ripe to speak about yet.

6. THE OEDIPUS COMPLEX

340   After what I have told you about our method you may have gained rather more confidence in its scientific character, and will be inclined to agree that the fantasies which have been brought to light by psychoanalytic research are not just the arbitrary suppositions and illusions of psychoanalysts. Perhaps you will even be willing to listen patiently to what these products of unconscious fantasy can tell us.

341   The fantasies of adults are, in so far as they are conscious, immensely varied and take the most strongly individual forms. It is therefore impossible to give a general description of them. But it is very different when we enter by means of analysis into the world of unconscious fantasies. The diversity of the fantasy-material is indeed very great, but we do not find nearly so many individual peculiarities as in the conscious realm. We meet here with more typical material which is not infrequently repeated in similar form in different individuals. Constantly recurring in these fantasies are ideas which are variations of those found in religion and mythology. This fact is so striking that we may say we have discovered in these fantasies the forerunners of religious and mythological ideas.

342   I should have to enter into very much more detail to give you any adequate examples. For these problems I must refer you to my book *Symbols of Transformation*. Here I will only mention that the central symbol of Christianity—sacrifice—plays an important part in the fantasies of the unconscious. The Viennese school knows this phenomenon under the ambiguous name of "castration complex." This paradoxical use of the term follows from the special attitude of the Viennese school towards the question of sexuality, which I discussed earlier. I have devoted special attention to the problem of sacrifice in the above-mentioned book. I must content myself with this passing reference and will now proceed to say something about the origin of unconscious fantasies.

69

343   In a child's unconscious the fantasies are very much simpler, as if scaled to the childish milieu. Thanks to the concerted efforts of the psychoanalytic school, we have discovered that the most frequent fantasy of childhood is the so-called Oedipus complex. This term, too, seems the most unsuitable one possible. We all know that the tragic fate of Oedipus consisted in his marrying his mother and slaying his father. This tragic conflict of adult life appears far removed from the psyche of a child, and to the layman it seems quite inconceivable that a child should suffer from this conflict. But, with a little reflection, it will become clear that the *tertium comparationis* lies precisely in the *narrow restriction of the fate of Oedipus to his two parents.* This restriction is characteristic of the child, for the fate of the adult is not limited to the parents. To that extent Oedipus is the exponent of an infantile conflict magnified to adult proportions. The term "Oedipus complex" naturally does not mean conceiving this conflict in its adult form, but rather on a reduced scale suitable to childhood. All it means, in effect, is that the childish demands for love are directed to mother and father, and to the extent that these demands have already attained a certain degree of intensity, so that the chosen object is jealously defended, we can speak of an "Oedipus complex."

344   This weakening and reduction in scale of the Oedipus complex should not be understood as a diminution of the total sum of affect, but as indicating the smaller share of sexual affect characteristic of a child. To make up for this, childish affects have that peculiar intensity which is characteristic of the sexual affect in adults. The little son would like to have his mother all to himself and to be rid of his father. As you know, small children can sometimes force themselves between the parents in the most jealous way. In the unconscious these wishes and intentions assume a more concrete and more drastic form. Children are small primitive creatures and are therefore quickly ready to kill—a thought which is all the easier in the unconscious, because the unconscious is wont to express itself very dramatically. But as a child is, in general, harmless, this seemingly dangerous wish is as a rule harmless too. I say "as a rule," for we know that children can occasionally give way to their murderous impulses, not only indirectly, but in quite direct fashion. But just as the child is incapable of making systematic plans, so his intention to murder

70

is not all that dangerous. The same is true of his Oedipal intention towards the mother. The faint hints of this fantasy in the child's consciousness can easily be overlooked; all parents are therefore convinced that their children have no Oedipus complex. Parents, like lovers, are mostly blind. If I now say that the Oedipus complex is in the first place only a formula for childish desires in regard to the parents and for the conflict which these desires evoke—as every selfish desire must—the matter may seem more acceptable.

345   The history of the Oedipus fantasy is of special interest because it teaches us a great deal about the development of unconscious fantasies in general. People naturally think that the Oedipus problem is the problem of the son. But this, remarkably enough, is an illusion. Under certain conditions, the sexual libido reaches its final differentiation, corresponding to the sex of the individual, only relatively late in puberty. Before this time it has a sexually undifferentiated character, which could also be termed bisexual. It is therefore not surprising if little girls have an Oedipus complex too. So far as we know, the first love of a child, regardless of sex, belongs to the mother. If the love for the mother is intense at this stage, the father is jealously kept away as a rival. Of course, for the child itself, the mother at this early stage of childhood has no sexual significance worth mentioning, and to that extent the term "Oedipus complex" is not really suitable. At this period the mother still has the significance of a protecting, enfolding, nourishing being, who for this reason is a source of pleasure.

346   ⟨It is characteristic, too, that the babyish word for mother, "mamma," is the name for the maternal breast. As Dr. Beatrice Hinkle has informed me, interrogation of small children elicited the fact that they defined "mother" as the person who gives food, chocolate, etc. One could hardly assert that for children of this age food is only a symbol for sex, though this is sometimes true of adults. A superficial glance at the history of civilization will show just how enormous the nutritive source of pleasure is. The colossal feasts of Rome in its decadence were an expression of anything you like, only not of repressed sexuality, for that is the last thing one could accuse the Romans of in those days. There is no doubt that these excesses were some kind of substitute, but not for sexuality; they were far more a

substitute for neglected moral functions, which we are too prone to regard as laws forced on man from outside. Men have the laws which they make for themselves.)

347   As I explained earlier, I do not identify the feeling of pleasure *eo ipso* with sexuality. Sexuality has an increasingly small share in pleasure-sensations the further back we go in childhood. Nevertheless, jealousy can play a large role, for it too is something that does not belong entirely to the sexual sphere, since the desire for food has itself much to do with the first stirrings of jealousy—one has only to think of animals! Certainly it is reinforced by a budding eroticism relatively early. This element gains in strength as the years go on, so that the Oedipus complex soon assumes its classical form. The conflict takes on a more masculine and therefore more typical form in a son, whereas a daughter develops a specific liking for the father, with a correspondingly jealous attitude towards the mother. We could call this the Electra complex. As everyone knows, Electra took vengeance on her mother Clytemnestra for murdering her husband Agamemnon and thus robbing her—Electra—of her beloved father.

348   Both these fantasy complexes become more pronounced with increasing maturity, and reach a new stage only in the post-pubertal period, when the problem arises of detachment from the parents. This stage is characterized by the symbol we have already mentioned: the symbol of sacrifice. The more sexuality develops, the more it drives the individual away from his family and forces him to achieve independence. But the child has become closely attached to the family by his whole previous history, and especially to the parents, so that it is often only with the greatest difficulty that the growing individual can free himself inwardly from his infantile milieu. If he does not succeed in this, the Oedipus (or Electra) complex will precipitate a conflict, and then there is the possibility of neurotic disturbances. The libido, already sexually developed, pours into the Oedipal "mould" and gives rise to feelings and fantasies which prove beyond doubt the effectiveness of the complex, which till then had been unconscious and more or less inoperative.

349   The first consequence is the formation of intense resistances against the "immoral" impulses stemming from the now active complex. This affects the conscious behaviour in two ways.

Either the consequences are direct, in which case the son displays violent resistances against his father and a particularly affectionate and dependent attitude towards his mother; or they are indirect, that is to say compensated: instead of resistance to the father there is marked submissiveness coupled with an irritated, antagonistic attitude towards the mother. Direct and compensated consequences can sometimes alternate. All this is true also of the Electra complex. If the sexual libido were to get stuck in this form, the Oedipus and Electra conflict would lead to murder and incest. This naturally does not happen with normal people, nor in so-called "amoral" primitive communities, otherwise the human race would have perished long ago. On the contrary, it is in the natural order of things that familiar objects lose their compelling charm and force the libido to seek new objects; and this acts as an important regulative factor which prevents parricide and incest. The continuous development of libido towards objects outside the family is perfectly normal and natural, and it is an abnormal and pathological phenomenon if the libido remains, as it were, glued to the family. Nevertheless, it is a phenomenon that can sometimes be observed in normal people.

THE PROBLEM OF INCEST

350   ⟨The unconscious fantasy of sacrifice, occurring some time after puberty, is a direct outcome of the infantile complexes. Of this I have given a circumstantial example in my book *Symbols of Transformation*. The fantasy of sacrifice means the giving up of infantile wishes. I have shown this in my book and at the same time have pointed out the parallels in the history of religion. It is not surprising that this problem plays an important role in religion, for religion is one of the greatest helps in the psychological process of adaptation. The chief obstacle to new modes of psychological adaptation is conservative adherence to the earlier attitude. But man cannot leave his previous personality and his previous objects of interest simply as they are, otherwise his libido would stagnate in the past, and this would be an impoverishment for him. Here religion is a great help because, by the bridge of the symbol, it leads his

73

libido away from the infantile objects (parents) towards the symbolic representatives of the past, i.e., the gods, thus facilitating the transition from the infantile world to the adult world. In this way the libido is set free for social purposes.)

351   Freud has a special conception of the incest complex which has given rise to heated controversy. He starts from the fact that the Oedipus complex is usually unconscious, and he conceives this to be the consequence of a moral repression. It is possible that I am not expressing myself quite correctly if I give you Freud's view in these words. At any rate, according to him the Oedipus complex seems to be repressed, that is, displaced into the unconscious through the reactive effect of conscious tendencies. It almost looks as if the Oedipus complex would rise to consciousness if the child's development were uninhibited and were not affected by cultural influences.[1]

352   Freud calls the barrier that prevents this acting out of the Oedipus complex the "incest barrier." He seems to believe, so far as one can gather from his writings, that the incest barrier is formed by the backwash of experience, that it is a correction by reality, since the unconscious strives for boundless and immediate satisfaction without regard for others. In this he agrees with Schopenhauer, who says of the egoism of the blind World-Will that it is so strong that a man could slay his brother merely to grease his boots with his brother's fat. Freud considers that the psychological incest barrier can be compared with the incest prohibitions found even among primitives. He further considers that these prohibitions are a proof that men really do desire incest, for which reason laws were framed against it even on the primitive level. He therefore takes the tendency towards incest to be an absolutely concrete sexual wish, for he calls this complex the root-complex, or nucleus, of the neuroses and is inclined, viewing this as the original one, to reduce practically the whole psychology of the neuroses, as well as many other phenomena in the realm of the mind, to this one complex.

[1] A view expressed most strongly by Stekel.

7. THE AETIOLOGY OF NEUROSIS

353   With this new conception of Freud's we come back to the question of the aetiology of neurosis. We have seen that psychoanalytic theory started from a traumatic experience in childhood, which later on was found to be partly or wholly unreal. In consequence, the theory made a change of front and sought the aetiologically significant factor in the development of abnormal fantasies. The investigation of the unconscious, continued over a period of ten years with the help of an increasing number of workers, gradually brought to light a mass of empirical material which showed that the incest complex was a highly important and never-failing element in pathological fantasy. But it was found that the incest complex was not a special complex of neurotic people; it proved to be a component of the normal infantile psyche. We cannot tell from its mere existence whether this complex will give rise to a neurosis or not. To become pathogenic, it must precipitate a conflict; the complex, which in itself is inactive, must be activated and intensified to the point where a conflict breaks out.

354   This brings us to a new and important question. If the infantile "nuclear complex" is only a general form, not in itself pathogenic but requiring special activation, then the whole aetiological problem is altered. In that case we would dig in vain among the reminiscences of earliest childhood, since they give us only the general forms of later conflicts but not the actual conflict. (It makes no difference that there were already conflicts in childhood, for the conflicts of childhood are different from the conflicts of adults. Those who have suffered ever since childhood from a chronic neurosis do not suffer now from the same conflict they suffered from then. Maybe the neurosis broke out when they first had to go to school as children. Then it was the conflict between indulgence and duty, between love for their parents and the necessity of going to school. But now it is the conflict between, say, the joys of a

75

comfortable bourgeois existence and the strenuous demands of professional life. It only seems to be the same conflict. It is just as if the "Teutschen" of the Napoleonic wars were to compare themselves with the old Germans who rebelled against the Roman yoke.)

UNCONSCIOUS DETERMINATION

355   I think I can best make my meaning clear if I describe the subsequent development of the theory by using the example of the young lady whose story you have heard in the earlier lectures. As you will probably remember, we found in the anamnesis that the fright with the horses led to the reminiscence of a similar scene in childhood, in which connection we discussed the trauma theory. We found that we had to look for the real pathological element in her exaggerated fantasies, which arose from her retarded psychosexual development. We now have to apply the theoretical insight we have thus gained to the genesis of this particular illness if we want to understand how, just at that moment, that childhood experience was constellated so effectively.

356   The simplest way to find an explanation for that nocturnal occurrence would be to make an exact inquiry into the circumstances of the moment. The first thing I did, therefore, was to question the patient about the company she had been keeping at the time. From this I learnt that she knew a young man to whom she thought of getting engaged; she loved him and hoped to be happy with him. At first nothing more could be discovered. But it would never do to be deterred from investigation by the negative results of the preliminary questioning. There are indirect ways of reaching the goal when the direct way fails. We therefore return to that singular moment when the lady ran headlong in front of the horses. We inquire about her companions and the sort of festive occasion she had just taken part in. It had been a farewell party for her best friend, who was going abroad to a health-resort on account of her nerves. This friend was married and, we are told, happily; she was also the mother of a child. We may take leave to doubt the statement that she was happy; for, were she really so, she would

76

presumably have no reason to be "nervous" and in need of a cure.

357   Shifting my angle of approach, I learnt that after her friends had caught up with her they took the patient back to the house of her host, as this was the nearest shelter. There she was hospitably received in her exhausted state. At this point the patient broke off her narrative, became embarrassed, fidgeted, and tried to change the subject. Evidently some disagreeable recollection had suddenly bobbed up. After the most obstinate resistance had been overcome, it appeared that yet another very remarkable incident had occurred that night: the amiable host had made her a fiery declaration of love, thus precipitating a situation which, in the absence of the lady of the house, might well be considered both difficult and distressing. Ostensibly this declaration of love came to her like a bolt from the blue. A modicum of criticism teaches us, however, that these things never drop from the skies but always have their history. It was now the task of the next few weeks to dig out bit by bit a long love-story, until at last a complete picture emerged which I attempt to outline as follows:

358   As a child the patient had been a regular tomboy, caring only for wild boys' games, scorning her own sex and avoiding all feminine ways and occupations. After puberty, when the erotic problem might have come too close, she began to shun all society, hated and despised everything that even remotely reminded her of the biological destiny of woman, and lived in a world of fantasy which had nothing in common with rude reality. Thus, until about her twenty-fourth year, she evaded all those little adventures, hopes, and expectations which ordinarily move a girl's heart at this age. Then she got to know two men who were destined to break through the thorny hedge that had grown up around her. Mr. A was her best friend's husband, and Mr. B was his bachelor friend. She liked them both. Nevertheless it soon began to look as though she liked Mr. B a vast deal better. An intimacy quickly sprang up between them and before long there was talk of a possible engagement. Through her relations with Mr. B and through her friend she often came into contact with Mr. A, whose presence sometimes disturbed her in the most unaccountable way and made her nervous.

77

359 About this time the patient went to a large party. Her friends were also there. She became lost in thought and was dreamily playing with her ring when it suddenly slipped off her finger and rolled under the table. Both gentlemen looked for it and Mr. B succeeded in finding it. He placed the ring on her finger with an arch smile and said, "You know what that means!" Overcome by a strange and irresistible feeling, she tore the ring from her finger and flung it through the open window. A painful moment ensued, as may be imagined, and soon she left the party in deep dejection.

360 Not long after this, so-called chance brought it about that she should spend her summer holidays at a health resort where Mr. and Mrs. A were also staying. Mrs. A then began to grow visibly nervous, and frequently stayed indoors because she felt out of sorts. The patient was thus in a position to go out for walks alone with Mr. A. On one occasion they went boating. So boisterous was she in her merriment that she suddenly fell overboard. She could not swim, and it was only with great difficulty that Mr. A pulled her half-unconscious into the boat. And then it was that he kissed her. With this romantic episode the bonds were tied fast. To excuse herself in her own eyes she tried all the more energetically to get herself engaged to Mr. B, telling herself every day that it was Mr. B whom she really loved. Naturally this curious little game had not escaped the keen glances of wifely jealousy. Mrs. A, her friend, had guessed the secret and fretted accordingly, so that her nerves only got worse. Hence it became necessary for Mrs. A to go abroad for a cure.[1]

361 The farewell party presented a dangerous opportunity. The patient knew that her friend and rival was going off the same evening, and that Mr. A would be alone in the house. Of course she did not think this out logically and clearly, for some women have a remarkable capacity for thinking purely with their feelings, and not with their intellects, so that it seems to them as if they had never thought certain things at all. At any rate she had a very queer feeling all the evening. She felt extraordinarily nervous, and when Mrs. A had been accompanied to the station and had gone, the hysterical twilight state came over her on the

[1] [Cf. *Two Essays*, pars. 11f. and 420. For the first two instalments of the story see supra, pars. 218ff. and 297ff.—EDITORS.]

78

way back. I asked her what she had been thinking or feeling at the actual moment when she heard the horses coming along behind her. Her answer was that she had only a feeling of panic, the feeling that something dreadful was approaching which she could no longer escape. The consequence was, as you know, that she was brought back exhausted to the house of her host, Mr. A.

362   To the simple mind this dénouement seems perfectly obvious. Every layman will say, "Well, that is clear enough, she only intended to return by one way or another to Mr. A's house." But the psychologist would reproach the layman for his incorrect way of expressing himself, and would tell him that the patient was not conscious of the motives of her behaviour, and that we cannot therefore speak of her *intention* to return to Mr. A's house. There are, of course, learned psychologists who could find any number of theoretical reasons for disputing the purposiveness of her action—reasons based on the dogma of the identity of consciousness and psyche. But the psychology inaugurated by Freud recognized long ago that the purposive significance of psychological acts cannot be judged by conscious motives but only by the objective criterion of their psychological result. Today it can no longer be contested that there are unconscious tendencies which have a great influence on a person's reactions and on the effect he has on others.

363   What happened at Mr. A's house bears out this observation. Our patient made a sentimental scene, and Mr. A felt obliged to react to it with a declaration of love. Looked at in the light of these concluding events, the whole previous history seems to be very ingeniously directed towards precisely this end, though consciously the patient was struggling against it all the time.

364   The theoretical gain from this story is the clear recognition that an unconscious "intention" or tendency stage-managed the fright with the horses, very probably using for this purpose the infantile reminiscence of the horses galloping irresistibly towards disaster. Seen in the light of the whole material, the nocturnal scene with the horses—the starting point of the illness—seems to be only the keystone of a planned edifice. The fright and the apparently traumatic effect of the childhood experience are merely staged, but staged in the peculiar way characteristic of hysteria, so that the *mise en scène* appears almost exactly

79

like a reality. We know from hundreds of experiences that hysterical pains are staged in order to reap certain advantages from the environment. Nevertheless these pains are entirely real. The patients do not merely think they have pains; from the psychological point of view the pains are just as real as those due to organic causes, and yet they are stage-managed.

THE REGRESSION OF LIBIDO

365   This utilization of reminiscences for staging an illness or an ostensible aetiology is called a *regression of libido*. The libido goes back to these reminiscences and activates them, with the result that an apparent aetiology is simulated. In this instance, according to the old theory, it might seem as if the fright with the horses were due to the old trauma. The resemblance between the two scenes is unmistakable, and in both cases the patient's fright was very real. At all events, we have no reason to doubt her assertions in this respect, as they fully accord with our experiences of other patients. The nervous asthma, the hysterical anxiety-attacks, the psychogenic depressions and exaltations, the pains, the cramps, etc. are all quite real, and any doctor who has himself suffered from a psychogenic symptom will know how absolutely real it feels. Regressively reactivated reminiscences, however fantastic they may be, are as real as recollections of events which have actually happened.

366   As the term "regression of libido" indicates, we understand by this retrograde mode of application a reversion to earlier stages. From our example we can see very clearly how the process of regression takes place. At that farewell party, which presented a good opportunity for her to be alone with her host, the patient shrank from the idea of turning this opportunity to her advantage, but let herself be overpowered by desires which hitherto she had never admitted. The libido was not used consciously for that purpose, nor was this purpose ever acknowledged. In consequence, the libido had to carry it out by means of the unconscious, under the cover of panic in face of overwhelming danger. Her feelings at the moment when the horses approached illustrate our formulation very clearly: she felt as if something inescapable now had to happen.

367   The process of regression is beautifully illustrated in an image used by Freud. The libido can be compared with a river which, when it meets with an obstruction, gets dammed up and causes an inundation. If this river has previously, in its upper reaches, dug out other channels, these channels will be filled up again by reason of the damming below. They appear to be real river-beds, filled with water as before, but at the same time they have only a provisional existence. The river has not permanently flowed back into the old channels, but only for as long as the obstruction lasts in the main stream. The subsidiary streams carry the water not because they were independent streams from the beginning, but because they were once stages or stations in the development of the main river-bed, passing possibilities, traces of which still exist and can therefore be used again in times of flood.

368   This image can be applied directly to the development of the uses of libido. The final direction, the main river-bed, has not yet been found at the time of the infantile development of sexuality. Instead, the libido branches out into all sorts of subsidiary streams, and only gradually does the final form appear. But when the river has dug out its main bed, all the subsidiary streams dry up and lose their importance, leaving only traces of their former activity. Similarly, the importance of the child's preliminary exercises at sexuality disappears almost completely as a rule, except for a few traces. If later an obstruction occurs, so that the damming up of libido reactivates the old channels, this state is properly speaking a new and at the same time an abnormal one. The earlier, infantile state represents a normal application of libido, whereas the reversion of libido to infantile ways is something abnormal. I am therefore of the opinion that Freud is not justified in calling the infantile sexual manifestations "perverse," since a normal manifestation should not be designated by a pathological term. This incorrect usage has had pernicious consequences in confusing the scientific public. Such a terminology is a misapplication to normal people of insights gained from neurotic psychology, on the assumption that the abnormal by-path taken by the libido in neurotics is still the same phenomenon as in children.

369   The so-called "amnesia of childhood," which I would like to mention in passing, is a similar illegitimate "retrograde" appli-

cation of terms from pathology. Amnesia is a pathological condition, consisting in the repression of certain conscious contents, and this cannot possibly be the same as the anterograde amnesia of children, which consists in an incapacity for intentional memory-reproduction, such as is also found among primitives. This incapacity for memory-reproduction dates from birth and can be understood on quite obvious biological grounds. It would be a remarkable hypothesis if we were to assume that this totally different quality of infantile consciousness could be reduced to sexual repressions on the analogy of a neurosis. A neurotic amnesia is punched out, as it were, from the continuity of memory, whereas memory in early childhood consists of single islands in the continuum of non-memory. This condition is in every sense the opposite of the condition found in neurosis, so that the expression "amnesia" is absolutely incorrect. The "amnesia of childhood" is an inference from the psychology of neurosis, just as is the "polymorphous-perverse" disposition of the child.

THE PERIOD OF SEXUAL LATENCY

370   This error in theoretical formulation comes to light in the peculiar doctrine of the so-called "period of sexual latency" in childhood. Freud observed that the early infantile sexual manifestations, which I call phenomena of the presexual stage, disappear after a time and reappear only much later. What Freud calls "infantile masturbation"—that is, all those quasi-sexual activities which we spoke about before—is said to return later as real masturbation. Such a process of development would be biologically unique. In conformity with this theory we would have to assume, for instance, that when a plant forms a bud from which a blossom begins to unfold, the blossom is taken back again before it is fully developed, and is again hidden within the bud, to reappear later on in a similar form. This impossible supposition is a consequence of the assertion that the early infantile activities of the presexual stage are sexual phenomena, and that the quasi-masturbational acts of that period are genuine acts of masturbation. Here the incorrect terminology and the boundless extension of the concept of sexuality take their

revenge. Thus it was that Freud was compelled to assume that there is a disappearance of sexuality, in other words, a period of sexual latency. What he calls a disappearance is nothing other than the *real beginning of sexuality*, everything preceding it being but a preliminary stage to which no real sexual character can be attributed. The impossible phenomenon of sexual latency is thus explained in a very simple way.

371 The theory of the latency period is an excellent example of the incorrectness of the conception of infantile sexuality. But there has been no error of observation. On the contrary, the hypothesis of the latency period proves how exactly Freud observed the apparent recommencement of sexuality. The error lies in the conception. As we have already seen, the prime error consists in a somewhat old-fashioned conception of a plurality of instincts. As soon as we accept the idea of two or more instincts existing side by side, we must necessarily conclude that, if one instinct is not yet manifest, it is still present *in nuce,* in accordance with the old theory of encasement.[2] Or, in physics, we should have to say that when a piece of iron passes from the condition of heat to the condition of light, the light was already present *in nuce* (latently) in the heat. Such assumptions are arbitrary projections of human ideas into transcendental regions, contravening the requirements of the theory of cognition. We have therefore no right to speak of a sexual instinct existing *in nuce,* as we would then be giving an arbitrary interpretation of phenomena which can be explained otherwise, in a much more suitable manner. We can only speak of the manifestation of the nutritive function, of the sexual function, and so on, and then only when that function has come to the surface with unmistakable clarity. We speak of light only when the iron is visibly glowing, but not when the iron is merely hot.

372 Freud as an observer sees quite clearly that the sexuality of neurotics cannot really be compared with infantile sexuality, just as there is a great difference, for instance, between the uncleanliness of a two-year-old child and the uncleanliness of a forty-year-old catatonic. The one is normal, the other exceedingly

2 [*Einschachtelung:* "An old theory of reproduction which assumed that when the first animal of each species was created, the germs of all other individuals of the same species which were to come from it were encased in its ova."—*Century Dictionary* (1890).—TRANS.]

pathological. Freud inserted a short passage in his *Three Essays*,[3] stating that the infantile form of neurotic sexuality is either wholly, or at any rate partly, due to regression. That is, even in those cases where we can say that it is still the same old infantile by-path, the function of this by-path is intensified by the regression. Freud thus admits that the infantile sexuality of neurotics is for the greater part a regressive phenomenon. That this must be so is evidenced by the researches of recent years, showing that the observations concerning the childhood psychology of neurotics hold equally true of normal people. At any rate we can say that the historical development of infantile sexuality in a neurotic is distinguished from that of normal people only by minimal differences which completely elude scientific evaluation. Striking differences are exceptional.

THE AETIOLOGICAL SIGNIFICANCE OF THE ACTUAL PRESENT

373   The more deeply we penetrate into the heart of the infantile development, the more we get the impression that as little of aetiological significance can be found there as in the infantile trauma. Even with the acutest ferreting into their respective histories we shall never discover why people living on German soil had just such a fate, and why the Gauls another. The further we get away, in analytical investigations, from the epoch of the manifest neurosis, the less can we expect to find the real *causa efficiens,* since the dynamics of the maladjustment grow fainter and fainter the further we go back into the past. In constructing a theory which derives the neurosis from causes in the distant past, we are first and foremost following the tendency of our patients to lure us as far away as possible from the critical present. *For the cause of the pathogenic conflict lies mainly in the present moment.* It is just as if a nation were to blame its miserable political conditions on the past; as if the Germany of the nineteenth century had attributed her political dismemberment and incapacity to her oppression by the Romans, instead of seeking the causes of her difficulties in the actual present. It is mainly in the present that the effective causes lie, and here alone are the possibilities of removing them.

3 Standard Edn., p. 232.

374   The greater part of the psychoanalytic school is still under the spell of the conception that infantile sexuality is the *sine qua non* of neurosis. It is not only the theorist, delving into childhood simply from scientific interest, but the practising analyst also, who believes that he has to turn the history of infancy inside out in order to find the fantasies conditioning the neurosis. A fruitless enterprise! In the meantime the most important factor escapes him, namely, the conflict and its demands in the present. In the case we have been describing, we should not understand any of the motives which produced the hysterical attacks if we looked for them in earliest childhood. Those reminiscences determine only the form, but the dynamic element springs from the present, and insight into the significance of the actual moment alone gives real understanding.

375   It may not be out of place to remark here that it would never occur to me to blame Freud personally for the innumerable misunderstandings. I know very well that Freud, being an empiricist, always publishes only provisional formulations to which he certainly does not attribute any eternal value. But it is equally certain that the scientific public is inclined to make a creed out of them, a system which is asserted as blindly on the one hand as it is attacked on the other. I can only say that from the sum total of Freud's writings certain average conceptions have crystallized out, which both sides treat far too dogmatically. These views have led to a number of undoubtedly incorrect technical axioms the existence of which cannot be postulated with any certainty in Freud's own work. We know that in the mind of a creator of new ideas things are much more fluid and flexible than they are in the minds of his followers. They do not possess his vital creativity, and they make up for this deficiency by a dogmatic allegiance, in exactly the same way as their opponents, who, like them, cling to the dead letter because they cannot grasp its living content. My words are thus addressed less to Freud, who I know recognizes to some extent the final orientation of the neuroses, than to his public, who continue to argue about his views.

376   From what has been said it should be clear that we gain insight into the history of a neurosis only when we understand that each separate element in it serves a purpose. We can now understand why that particular element in the previous history

of our case was pathogenic, and we also understand why it was chosen as a symbol. Through the concept of regression, the theory is freed from the narrow formula of the importance of childhood experiences, and the actual conflict acquires the significance which, on the empirical evidence, implicitly belongs to it. Freud himself introduced the concept of regression, as I have said, in his *Three Essays,* rightly acknowledging that experience does not permit us to seek the cause of a neurosis exclusively in the past. If it is true, then, that reminiscences become effective again chiefly because of regressive activation, we have to consider whether the apparently determining effects of the reminiscences can be traced back solely to the regression of libido.

377   As you have heard already, Freud himself in the *Three Essays* gives us to understand that the infantilism of neurotic sexuality is for the most part due to regression. This statement deserves considerably more emphasis than it received there. (Actually Freud did give it due emphasis in his later works.) The point is that the *regression of libido abolishes to a very large extent the aetiological significance of childhood experiences.* It had seemed to us very peculiar anyway that the Oedipus or Electra complex should have a determining influence in the formation of a neurosis, since these complexes are actually present in everyone, even in people who have never known their father and mother and were brought up by foster-parents. I have analysed cases of this kind, and found that the incest complex was as well developed in them as in other patients. This seems to me a good proof that the incest complex is much less a reality than a purely regressive fantasy formation, and that the conflicts resulting from it must be reduced rather to an anachronistic clinging to the infantile attitude than to real incestuous wishes, which are merely a cover for regressive fantasies. Looked at from this point of view, childhood experiences have a significance for neurosis only when they are made significant by a regression of libido. That this must be so to a very large extent is shown by the fact that neither the infantile sexual trauma nor the incest complex present in everyone causes hysteria. Neurosis occurs only when the incest complex is activated by regression.

86

FAILURE OF ADAPTATION

378   This brings us to the question: why does the libido become regressive? In order to answer this, we must examine more closely the conditions under which a regression arises. In discussing this problem with my patients I generally give the following example: A mountain-climber, attempting the ascent of a certain peak, happens to meet with an insurmountable obstacle, for instance a precipitous rock-face whose ascent is a sheer impossibility. After vainly seeking another route, he will turn back and regretfully abandon the idea of climbing that peak. He will say to himself: "It is not in my power to get over this difficulty, so I will climb an easier mountain."

379   Here we see a normal utilization of libido: the man turns back when he meets an insurmountable difficulty, and uses his libido, which could not attain its original goal, for the ascent of another mountain.

380   Now let us imagine that the rock-face was not really unclimbable so far as the man's physical abilities were concerned, but that he shrank back from this difficult undertaking from sheer funk. In this case two possibilities are open:

    1. The man will be annoyed by his own cowardice and will set out to prove himself less timid on another occasion, or perhaps he will admit that with his timidity he ought never to undertake such daring ascents. At any rate, he will acknowledge that his moral capacity is not sufficient to overcome the difficulties. He therefore uses the libido which did not attain its original aim for the useful purpose of self-criticism, and for evolving a plan by which he may yet be able, with due regard to his moral capacity, to realize his wish to climb a mountain.

    2. The second possibility is that the man does not admit his cowardice, and flatly asserts that the rock face is physically unclimbable, although he can very well see that, with sufficient courage, the obstacle could be overcome. But he prefers to deceive himself. This creates the psychological situation which is of significance for our problem.

381   At bottom the man knows perfectly well that it would be physically possible to overcome the difficulty, and that he is simply morally incapable of doing so. But he pushes this thought

aside because of its disagreeable character. He is so conceited that he cannot admit his cowardice. He brags about his courage and prefers to declare that things are impossible rather than that his own courage is inadequate. In this way he falls into contradiction with himself: on the one hand he has a correct appreciation of the situation, on the other he hides this knowledge from himself, behind the illusion of his bravery. He represses his correct insight and tries to force his subjective illusions on reality. The result of this contradiction is that his libido is split and the two halves fight one another. He pits his wish to climb the mountain against the opinion, invented by himself and supported by artificial arguments, that the mountain is unclimbable. He draws back not because of any real impossibility but because of an artificial barrier invented by himself. He has fallen into disunion with himself. From this moment on he suffers from an internal conflict. Now the realization of his cowardice gains the upper hand, now defiance and pride. In either case his libido is engaged in a useless civil war, and the man becomes incapable of any new enterprise. He will never realize his wish to climb a mountain, because he has gone thoroughly astray in the estimation of his moral qualities. His efficiency is reduced, he is not fully adapted, he has become—in a word—neurotic. The libido that retreated in face of the difficulty has led neither to honest self-criticism nor to a desperate struggle to overcome the difficulty at any price; it has been used merely to maintain the cheap pretence that the ascent was absolutely impossible and that even heroic courage would have availed nothing.

REVERSION TO THE INFANTILE LEVEL

382   This kind of reaction is called *infantile*. It is characteristic of children, and of naïve minds generally, not to find the mistake in themselves but in things outside them, and forcibly to impose on things their own subjective judgment.

383   This man, therefore, solves the problem in an infantile way; he substitutes for the adapted attitude of the first climber a mode of adaptation characteristic of the child's mind. That is what we mean by regression. His libido retreats before the ob-

stacle it cannot surmount and substitutes a childish illusion for real action.

384   Such cases are a daily occurrence in the treatment of neurosis. I would only remind you of all those young girls who suddenly become hysterically ill the moment they have to decide whether to get engaged or not. As an example, I will present the case of two sisters. The two girls were separated by only a year in age. In talents and also in character they were very much alike. They had the same education and grew up in the same surroundings under the same parental influences. Both were ostensibly healthy, neither showed any noticeable nervous symptoms. An attentive observer might have discovered that the elder daughter was rather more the darling of her parents than the younger. Her parents' esteem was due to the special kind of sensitiveness which this daughter displayed. She demanded more affection than the younger one, was somewhat more precocious and forthcoming than she. Besides, she showed some delightfully childish traits—just those things which, because of their contradictory and slightly unbalanced character, make a person specially charming. No wonder father and mother had great joy in their elder daughter.

385   When the two sisters became of marriageable age, they both made the acquaintance of two young men, and the possibility of their marriages soon drew near. As is generally the case, there were certain difficulties in the way. Both girls were quite young and had very little experience of the world. The men were fairly young too, and in positions which might have been better; they were only at the beginning of their careers, nevertheless both were capable young men. The two girls lived in social surroundings which gave them the right to certain expectations. It was a situation in which doubts as to the suitability of either marriage were permissible. Moreover, both girls were insufficiently acquainted with their prospective husbands, and were not quite sure of their love. Hence there were many hesitations and doubts. It was noticed that the elder sister always showed greater waverings in all her decisions. On account of these hesitations there were some painful moments with the two young men, who naturally pressed for a definite answer. At such moments the elder sister showed herself much more agitated than the younger one. Several times she went weeping to her mother, bemoaning

her own uncertainty. The younger one was more decided, and put an end to the unsettled situation by accepting her suitor. She thus got over her difficulty and thereafter events ran smoothly.

386   As soon as the admirer of the elder sister heard that the younger one had given her word, he rushed to his lady and begged passionately for her final acceptance. His tempestuous behaviour irritated and rather frightened her, although she was really inclined to follow her sister's example. She answered in a haughty and rather offhand way. He replied with sharp reproaches, causing her to answer still more tartly. At the end there was a tearful scene, and he went away in a huff. At home, he told the story to his mother, who expressed the opinion that the girl was obviously not the right one for him and that he had better choose someone else. The quarrel had made the girl profoundly doubtful whether she really loved him. It suddenly seemed to her impossible to leave her beloved parents and follow this man to an unknown destiny. Matters finally went so far that the relationship was broken off altogether. From then on the girl became moody; she showed unmistakable signs of the greatest jealousy towards her sister, but would neither see nor admit that she was jealous. The former happy relationship with her parents went to pieces too. Instead of her earlier child-like affection she put on a sulky manner, which sometimes amounted to violent irritability; weeks of depression followed. While the younger sister was celebrating her wedding, the elder went to a distant health-resort for nervous intestinal catarrh. I shall not continue the history of the illness; it developed into an ordinary hysteria.

387   In the analysis of this case great resistance was found to the sexual problem. The resistance was due to numerous perverse fantasies whose existence the patient would not admit. The question as to where these perverse fantasies, so unexpected in a young girl, could come from led to the discovery that once, as a child of eight years old, she had found herself suddenly confronted in the street by an exhibitionist. She was rooted to the spot by fright, and for a long time afterwards the ugly image pursued her in her dreams. Her younger sister had been with her at the time. The night after the patient told me about this, she dreamt of a man in a grey suit, who started to do in front of

90

her what the exhibitionist had done. She awoke with a cry of terror.

388   Her first association to the grey suit was a suit of her father's, which he had been wearing on an excursion she had made with him when she was about six years old. This dream, without any doubt, connects the father with the exhibitionist. There must be some reason for this. Did something happen with the father that might possibly call forth such an association? This question met with violent resistance from the patient, but it would not let her alone. At the next interview she reproduced some very early reminiscences, in which she had watched her father undressing; and one day she came, terribly embarrassed and shaken, to tell me that she had had an abominable vision, absolutely distinct. In bed at night, she suddenly felt herself once again a child of two or three years old, and she saw her father standing by her bed in an obscene attitude. The story was gasped out bit by bit, obviously with the greatest internal struggle. Then followed wild lamentations about how dreadful it was that a father should do such a terrible thing to his child.

389   Nothing is less probable than that the father really did this. It is only a fantasy, presumably constructed in the course of the analysis from that same need for causality which once misled the analysts into supposing that hysteria was caused merely by such impressions.

390   This case seems to me perfectly designed to demonstrate the importance of the regression theory, and to show at the same time the sources of the previous theoretical errors. Originally, as we saw, there was only a slight difference between the two sisters, but from the moment of their engagement their ways became totally divided. They now seemed to have two entirely different characters. The one, vigorous in health, and enjoying life, was a fine courageous girl, willing to submit to the natural demands of womanhood; the other was gloomy, ill-tempered, full of bitterness and malice, unwilling to make any effort to lead a reasonable life, egotistical, quarrelsome, and a nuisance to all around her. This striking difference was brought out only when one of the sisters successfully got over the difficulties of the engagement period, while the other did not. For both, it hung by a hair whether the affair would be broken off. The younger, somewhat more placid, was the more decided, and she

was able to find the right word at the right moment. The elder was more spoiled and more sensitive, consequently more influenced by her emotions, so that she could not find the right word, nor had she the courage to sacrifice her pride to put things straight afterwards. This little cause had a great effect, as we shall see. Originally the conditions were exactly the same for both sisters. It was the greater sensitiveness of the elder that made all the difference.

SENSITIVENESS AND REGRESSION

391   The question now is, whence came this sensitiveness which had such unfortunate results? Analysis demonstrated the existence of an extraordinarily well-developed sexuality with an infantile, fantastic character; further, of an incestuous fantasy about the father. Assuming that these fantasies had long been alive and active in the patient, we have here a quick and very simple solution of the problem of sensitiveness. We can easily understand why the girl was so sensitive: she was completely shut up in her fantasies and had a secret attachment to her father. In these circumstances it would have been a miracle if she had been willing to love and marry another man.

392   The further we pursue the development of these fantasies back to their source, following our need for causality, the greater become the difficulties of analysis, that is, the greater become the "resistances," as we called them. Finally we reach that impressive scene, that obscene act, whose improbability has already been established. This scene has exactly the character of a later fantasy-formation. Therefore, we have to conceive these difficulties, these "resistances," not—at least in this stage of the analysis—as defences against the conscious realization of a painful memory, but as a struggle against the construction of this fantasy.

393   You will ask in astonishment: But what is it that compels the patient to weave such a fantasy? You will even be inclined to suggest that the analyst forced the patient to invent it, otherwise she would never have produced such an absurd idea. I do not venture to doubt that there have been cases where the analyst's need to find a cause, especially under the influence of the

trauma theory, forced the patient to invent a fantasy of this kind. But the analyst, in his turn, would never have arrived at this theory had he not followed the patient's line of thought, thus taking part in that retrograde movement of libido which we call regression. He is simply carrying out to its logical conclusion what the patient is afraid to carry out, that is, a regression, a retreat of libido with all the consequences that this entails.

394   Hence, in tracing the libido regression, the analysis does not always follow the exact path marked out by the historical development, but often that of a subsequently formed fantasy, based only in part on former realities. In our case, too, the events were only partly real, and they got their enormous significance only afterwards, when the libido regressed. Whenever the libido seizes upon a certain reminiscence, we may expect it to be elaborated and transformed, for everything that is touched by the libido revives, takes on dramatic form, and becomes systematized. We have to admit that by far the greater part of the material became significant only later, when the regressing libido, seizing hold of anything suitable that lay in its path, had turned all this into a fantasy. Then that fantasy, keeping pace with the regressive movement of libido, came back at last to the father and put upon him all the infantile sexual wishes. Even so has it ever been thought that the golden age of Paradise lay in the past!

395   As we know that the fantasy material brought out by analysis became significant only afterwards, we are not in a position to use this material to explain the onset of the neurosis; we should be constantly moving in a circle. The critical moment for the neurosis was the one when the girl and the man were both ready to be reconciled, but when the inopportune sensitiveness of the patient, and perhaps also of her partner, allowed the opportunity to slip by.

IS SENSITIVENESS PRIMARY?

396   It might be said—and the psychoanalytic school inclines to this view—that the critical sensitiveness arose from a special psychological history which made this outcome a foregone conclu-

sion. We know that in psychogenic neuroses sensitiveness is always a symptom of disunion with oneself, a symptom of the struggle between two divergent tendencies. Each of these tendencies has its psychological prehistory, and in our case it can clearly be shown that the peculiar resistance at the bottom of the patient's critical sensitiveness was in fact bound up historically with certain infantile sexual activities, and also with that so-called traumatic experience—things which may very well cast a shadow on sexuality. This would be plausible enough, were it not that the patient's sister had experienced pretty much the same things—including the exhibitionist—without suffering the same consequences, and without becoming neurotic.

397   We would therefore have to assume that the patient experienced these things in a special way, perhaps more intensely and enduringly than her sister, and that the events of early childhood would have been more significant to her in the long run. If that had been true in so marked a degree, some violent effect would surely have been noticed even at the time. But in later youth the events of early childhood were as much over and done with for the patient as they were for her sister. Therefore, yet another conjecture is conceivable with regard to that critical sensitiveness, namely, that it did not come from her peculiar prehistory but had existed all along. An attentive observer of small children can detect, even in early infancy, any unusual sensitiveness. I once analysed a hysterical patient who showed me a letter written by her mother when the patient was two years old. Her mother wrote about her and her sister: she—the patient—was always a friendly and enterprising child, but her sister had difficulties in getting along with people and things. The first one in later life became hysterical, the other catatonic. These far-reaching differences, which go back into earliest childhood, cannot be due to accidental events but must be regarded as innate. From this standpoint we cannot assert that our patient's peculiar prehistory was to blame for her sensitiveness at the critical moment; it would be more correct to say that this sensitiveness was inborn and naturally manifested itself most strongly in any unusual situation.

398   This excessive sensitiveness very often brings an enrichment of the personality and contributes more to its charm than to the undoing of a person's character. Only, when difficult and un-

usual situations arise, the advantage frequently turns into a very great disadvantage, since calm consideration is then disturbed by untimely affects. Nothing could be more mistaken, though, than to regard this excessive sensitiveness as in itself a pathological character component. If that were really so, we should have to rate about one quarter of humanity as pathological. Yet if this sensitiveness has such destructive consequences for the individual, we must admit that it can no longer be considered quite normal.

399   We are driven to this contradiction when we contrast the two views concerning the significance of the psychological prehistory as sharply as we have done here. In reality, it is not a question of either one or the other. A certain innate sensitiveness produces a special prehistory, a special way of experiencing infantile events, which in their turn are not without influence on the development of the child's view of the world. Events bound up with powerful impressions can never pass off without leaving some trace on sensitive people. Some of them remain effective throughout life, and such events can have a determining influence on a person's whole mental development. Dirty and disillusioning experiences in the realm of sexuality are especially apt to frighten off a sensitive person for years afterwards, so that the mere thought of sex arouses the greatest resistances.

400   As the trauma theory shows, we are too much inclined, knowing of such cases, to attribute the emotional development of a person wholly, or at least very largely, to accidents. The old trauma theory went too far in this respect. We must never forget that the world is, in the first place, a subjective phenomenon. *The impressions we receive from these accidental happenings are also our own doing.* It is not true that the impressions are forced on us unconditionally; our own predisposition conditions the impression. A man whose libido is blocked will have, as a rule, quite different and very much more vivid impressions than one whose libido is organized in a wealth of activities. A person who is sensitive in one way or another will receive a deep impression from an event which would leave a less sensitive person cold.

401   Therefore, in addition to the accidental impression, we have to consider the subjective conditions seriously. Our previous

reflections, and in particular our discussion of an actual case, have shown that the most important subjective condition is regression. The effect of regression, as practical experience shows, is so great and so impressive that one might be inclined to attribute the effect of accidental occurrences solely to the mechanism of regression. Without any doubt, there are many cases where everything is dramatized, where even the traumatic experiences are pure figments of the imagination, and the few real events among them are afterwards completely distorted by fantastic elaboration. We can safely say that there is not a single case of neurosis in which the emotional value of the antecedent experience is not intensified by libido regression, and even when large tracts of infantile development seem to be extraordinarily significant (as for instance the relationship to the parents), it is almost always a regression that gives them this value.

402   The truth, as always, lies in the middle. The previous history certainly has a determining value, and this is intensified by regression. Sometimes the traumatic significance of the previous history comes more to the forefront, sometimes only its regressive meaning. These considerations naturally have to be applied to infantile sexual experiences as well. Obviously there are cases where brutal sexual experiences justify the shadow thrown on sexuality and make the later resistance to sex thoroughly comprehensible. (I would mention, by the way, that frightful impressions other than sexual can leave behind a permanent feeling of insecurity which may give the individual a hesitating attitude to reality.) Where real events of undoubted traumatic potency are absent—as is the case in most neuroses—the mechanism of regression predominates.

403   It might be objected that we have no criterion by which to judge the potential effect of a trauma, since this is an extremely relative concept. That is not altogether true; we have such a criterion in the average normal person. Something that is likely to make a strong and abiding impression on a normal person must be considered as having a determining influence for neurotics also. But we cannot attribute determining importance, in neurosis either, to impressions which normally would disappear and be forgotten. In most cases where some event has had an unexpected traumatic effect, we shall in all probability find a regression, that is to say, a secondary fantastic dramatization.

The earlier in childhood an impression is said to have arisen, the more suspect is its reality. Primitive people and animals have nothing like that capacity for reviving memories of unique impressions which we find among civilized people. Very young children are not nearly as impressionable as older children. The higher development of the mental faculties is an indispensable prerequisite for impressionability. We can therefore safely assume that the earlier a patient places some impressive experience in his childhood, the more likely it is to be a fantastic and regressive one. Deeper impressions are to be expected only from experiences in late childhood. At any rate, we generally have to attribute only regressive significance to the events of early infancy, that is, from the fifth year back. In later years, too, regression can sometimes play an overwhelming role, but even so one must not attribute too little importance to accidental events. In the later course of a neurosis, accidental events and regression together form a vicious circle: retreat from life leads to regression, and regression heightens resistance to life.

THE TELEOLOGICAL SIGNIFICANCE OF REGRESSION

404   ⟨Before pursuing our argument further, we must turn to the question of what teleological significance should be attributed to regressive fantasies. We might be satisfied with the hypothesis that these fantasies are simply a substitute for real action and therefore have no further significance. That can hardly be so. Psychoanalytic theory inclines to see the reason for the neurosis in the fantasies (illusions, prejudices, etc.), as their character betrays a tendency which is often directly opposed to reasonable action. Indeed, it often looks as if the patient were really using his previous history only to prove that he cannot act reasonably, whereupon the analyst, who, like everyone else, is easily inclined to sympathize with the patient (i.e., to identify with him unconsciously), gets the impression that the patient's arguments constitute a real aetiology. In other cases the fantasies have more the character of wonderful ideals which put beautiful and airy phantasms in the place of crude reality. Here a more or less obvious megalomania is always present, aptly compensating for the patient's indolence and deliberate incompetence. But the

97

decidedly sexual fantasies often reveal their purpose quite clearly, which is to accustom the patient to the thought of his sexual destiny, and so help him to overcome his resistance.

405   If we agree with Freud that neurosis is an unsuccessful attempt at self-cure, we must allow the fantasies, too, a double character: on one hand a pathological tendency to resist, on the other a helpful and preparatory tendency. With a normal person the libido, when it is blocked by an obstacle, forces him into a state of introversion and makes him reflect. So, too, with a neurotic under the same conditions: an introversion ensues, with increased fantasy activity. But he gets stuck there, because he prefers the infantile mode of adaptation as being the easier one. He does not see that he is exchanging his momentary advantage for a permanent disadvantage and has thus done himself a bad turn. In the same way, it is much easier and more convenient for the civic authorities to neglect all those troublesome sanitary precautions, but when an epidemic comes the sin of omission takes bitter revenge. If, therefore, the neurotic claims all manner of infantile alleviations, he must also accept the consequences. And if he is not willing to do so, then the consequences will overtake him.

406   It would, in general, be a great mistake to deny any teleological value to the apparently pathological fantasies of a neurotic. They are, as a matter of fact, the first beginnings of spiritualization, the first groping attempts to find new ways of adapting. His retreat to the infantile level does not mean only regression and stagnation, but also the possibility of discovering a new life-plan. Regression is thus in very truth the basic condition for the act of creation. Once again I must refer you to my oft-cited book *Symbols of Transformation.*)

8. THERAPEUTIC PRINCIPLES
OF PSYCHOANALYSIS

407   With the concept of regression, psychoanalysis made probably one of the most important discoveries in this field. Not
only were the earlier formulations of the genesis of neurosis
overthrown or at least considerably modified, but the *actual
conflict* received, for the first time, its proper valuation.

408   In our earlier case of the lady and the horses, we saw that the
symptomatological dramatization could only be understood
when it was seen as an expression of the actual conflict. Here
psychoanalytic theory joins hands with the results of the association experiments, of which I spoke in my lectures at Clark
University. The association experiment, when conducted on a
neurotic person, gives us a number of pointers to definite conflicts in his actual life, which we call complexes. These complexes contain just those problems and difficulties which have
brought the patient into disharmony with himself. Generally
we find a love-conflict of a quite obvious character. From the
standpoint of the association experiment, neurosis appears as
something quite different from what it seemed to be from the
standpoint of earlier psychoanalytic theory. From that standpoint, neurosis seemed to be a formation having its roots in
earliest infancy and overgrowing the normal psychic structure;
considered from the standpoint of the association experiment,
neurosis appears as a reaction to an actual conflict, which naturally is found just as often among normal people but is solved
by them without too much difficulty. The neurotic, however,
remains in the grip of the conflict, and his neurosis seems to be
more or less the consequence of his having got stuck. We can
say, therefore, that the results of the association experiment
argue strongly in favour of the regression theory.

99

• to become our own law giver, to be
autonomous
• ultimate priciple of morality
is duty

THE EVALUATION OF NEUROTIC FANTASIES

409   With the help of the earlier, "historical" conception of neurosis, we thought we could understand why a neurotic with a
powerful parental complex has such great difficulties in adapting himself to life. But now that we know that normal persons
have exactly the same complexes and, in principle, go through
the same psychological development as a neurotic, we can no
longer explain neurosis by the development of certain fantasy
systems. The really explanatory approach now is a prospective
one. We no longer ask whether the patient has a father or
mother complex, or unconscious incest fantasies which tie him
to his parents, for we know today that everybody has them. It
was a mistake to believe that only neurotics have such things.
We ask rather: What is the task which the patient does not
want to fulfil? What difficulty is he trying to avoid?

410   If a person tried always to adapt himself fully to the conditions of life, his libido would always be employed correctly and
adequately. When that does not happen, it gets blocked and
produces regressive symptoms. The non-fulfilment of the demands of adaptation, or the shrinking of the neurotic from difficulties, is, at bottom, the hesitation of every organism in the
face of a new effort to adapt. (The training of animals provides
instructive examples in this respect, and in many cases such an
explanation is, in principle, sufficient. From this standpoint
the earlier mode of explanation, which maintained that the
resistance of the neurotic was due to his bondage to fantasies,
appears incorrect. But it would be very one-sided to take our
stand solely on a point of principle. There is *also* a bondage to
fantasies, even though the fantasies are, as a rule, secondary.
The neurotic's bondage to fantasies (illusions, prejudices, etc.)
develops gradually, as a habit, out of innumerable regressions
from obstacles since earliest childhood. All this grows into a
regular habit familiar to every student of neurosis; we all know
those patients who use their neurosis as an excuse for running
away from difficulties and shirking their duty. Their habitual
evasion produces a habit of mind which makes them take it for
granted that they should live out their fantasies instead of fulfilling disagreeable obligations. And this bondage to fantasy

makes reality seem less real to the neurotic, less valuable and less interesting, than it does to the normal person. As I explained earlier, the fantastic prejudices and resistances may also arise, sometimes, from experiences that were not intended at all; in other words, were not deliberately sought disappointments and suchlike.)

411   The ultimate and deepest root of neurosis appears to be the innate sensitiveness,[1] which causes difficulties even to the infant at the mother's breast, in the form of unnecessary excitement and resistance. The apparent aetiology of neurosis elicited by psychoanalysis is actually, in very many cases, only an inventory of carefully selected fantasies, reminiscences, etc., aiming in a definite direction and created by the patient out of the libido he did not use for biological adaptation. Those allegedly aetiological fantasies thus appear to be nothing but substitute formations, disguises, artificial explanations for the failure to adapt to reality. The aforementioned vicious circle of flight from reality and regression into fantasy is naturally very apt to give the illusion of seemingly decisive causal relationships, which the analyst as well as the patient believes in. Accidental occurrences intervene in this mechanism only as "mitigating circumstances." Their real and effective existence must, however, be acknowledged.

412   I must admit that those critics are partly right who get the impression, from their reading of psychoanalytic case histories, that it is all fantastic and artificial. Only, they make the mistake of attributing the fantastic artefacts and lurid, far-fetched symbolisms to the suggestion and fertile imagination of the analyst, and not to the incomparably more fertile fantasy of his patients. In the fantasy material of a psychoanalytic case history there is, indeed, very much that is artificial. But the most striking thing is the active inventiveness of the patient. And the critics are not so wrong, either, when they say that their neurotic patients have no such fantasies. I do not doubt that most of their patients are totally unconscious of having any fantasies at all. When it is in the unconscious, a fantasy is "real" only when it has some demonstrable effect on consciousness, for instance in the form of a dream. Otherwise we can say with a clear conscience that it is

1 (Sensitiveness is naturally only one word for it. We could also say "reactivity" or "lability." As we know, there are many other words in circulation.)

not real. So anyone who overlooks the almost imperceptible effects of unconscious fantasies on consciousness, or dispenses with a thorough and technically irreproachable analysis of dreams, can easily overlook the fantasies of his patients altogether. We are therefore inclined to smile when we hear this oft-repeated objection.

413 Nevertheless, we must admit that there is some truth in it. The regressive tendency of the patient, reinforced by the attentions of the psychoanalyst in his examination of the unconscious fantasy activity, goes on inventing and creating even during the analysis. One could even say that this activity is greatly increased in the analytical situation, since the patient feels his regressive tendency strengthened by the interest of the analyst and produces even more fantasies than before. For this reason our critics have often remarked that a conscientious therapy of the neurosis should go in exactly the opposite direction to that taken by psychoanalysis; in other words, that it is the first task of therapy to extricate the patient from his unhealthy fantasies and bring him back again to real life.

414 The psychoanalyst, of course, is well aware of this, but he knows just how far one can go with this extricating of neurotics from their fantasies. As medical men, we should naturally never dream of preferring a difficult and complicated method, assailed by all the authorities, to a simple, clear, and easy one unless for a very good reason. I am perfectly well acquainted with hypnotic suggestion and Dubois' method of persuasion, but I do not use them because they are comparatively ineffective. For the same reason, I do not use "rééducation de la volonté" directly, as psychoanalysis gives me better results.

ACTIVE PARTICIPATION IN THE FANTASY

415 But, if we do use psychoanalysis, we must go along with the regressive fantasies of our patients. Psychoanalysis has a much broader outlook as regards the evaluation of symptoms than have the usual psychotherapeutic procedures. These all start from the assumption that neurosis is an entirely pathological formation. In the whole of neurology hitherto, no one has ever thought of seeing in the neurosis an attempt at healing, or, con-

sequently, of attributing to the neurotic formations a quite special teleological significance. But, like every illness, neurosis is only a compromise between the pathogenic causes and the normal function. Modern medicine no longer considers fever as the illness itself but as a purposive reaction of the organism. Similarly, psychoanalysis does not conceive the neurosis as anti-natural and in itself pathological, but as having a meaning and a purpose.

416   From this follows the inquiring and expectant attitude of psychoanalysis towards neurosis. In all cases it refrains from judging the value of a symptom, and tries instead to understand what tendencies lie beneath that symptom. If we were able to destroy a neurosis in the same way, for instance, as a cancer is destroyed, we would be destroying at the same time a large amount of useful energy. We save this energy, that is, we make it serve the purposes of the drive for recuperation, by pursuing the meaning of the symptoms and going along with the regressive movement of the patient. Those unfamiliar with the essentials of psychoanalysis will certainly have some difficulty in understanding how a therapeutic effect can be achieved when the analyst enters into the "harmful" fantasies of his patients. Not only the opponents of psychoanalysis but the patients themselves doubt the therapeutic value of such a method, which concentrates attention on the very things that the patient condemns as worthless and reprehensible, namely his fantasies. Patients will often tell you that their former doctors forbade them to have any concern with their fantasies, explaining that they could only consider themselves well when they were free, if only temporarily, from this terrible scourge. Naturally they wonder what good it will do when the treatment leads them back to the very place from which they consistently tried to escape.

417   This objection can be answered as follows: it all depends on the attitude the patient takes towards his fantasies. Hitherto, the patient's fantasying was a completely passive and involuntary activity. He was lost in his dreams, as we say. Even his so-called "brooding" was nothing but an involuntary fantasy. What psychoanalysis demands of the patient is apparently the same thing, but only a person with a very superficial knowledge of psychoanalysis could confuse this passive dreaming with the

attitude now required. What psychoanalysis asks of the patient is the exact opposite of what the patient has always done. He is like a man who has unintentionally fallen into the water and sunk, whereas psychoanalysis wants him to act like a diver. It was no mere chance which led him to fall in just at that spot. There lies the sunken treasure, but only a diver can bring it to the surface.

418   That is to say, when the patient judges them from a rational standpoint, he regards his fantasies as worthless and meaningless. In reality, however, they exert their great influence just because they are of such great importance. They are sunken treasures which can only be recovered by a diver; in other words the patient, contrary to his wont, must now deliberately turn his attention to his inner life. Where formerly he dreamed, he must now think, consciously and intentionally. This new way of thinking about himself has about as much resemblance to his former state of mind as a diver has to a drowning man. His former compulsion now has a meaning and a purpose, it has become *work*. The patient, assisted by the analyst, immerses himself in his fantasies, not in order to lose himself in them, but to salvage them, piece by piece, and bring them into the light of day. He thus acquires an objective vantage-point from which to view his inner life, and can now tackle the very thing he feared and hated. Here we have the basic principle of all psychoanalytic treatment.

understanding compulsion as fears

THE TASK OF ADAPTATION

419   Previously, because of his illness, the patient stood partly or wholly outside life. Consequently he neglected many of his duties, either in regard to social achievement or in regard to his purely human tasks. He must get back to fulfilling these duties if he wants to become well again. By way of caution, I would remark that "duties" are not to be understood here as general ethical postulates, but as duties to himself, by which again I do not mean egocentric interests—for a human being is also a social being, a fact too easily forgotten by individualists. A normal person feels very much more comfortable sharing a common virtue than possessing an individual vice, no matter how seduc-

tive it may be. He must already be a neurotic, or an otherwise unusual person, if he lets himself be deluded by special interests of this kind.

420   The neurotic shrank from his duties and his libido turned away, at least partly, from the tasks imposed by reality. Consequently it became introverted, directed towards his inner life. Because no attempt was made to master any real difficulties, his libido followed the path of regression, so that fantasy largely took the place of reality. Unconsciously—and very often consciously—the neurotic prefers to live in his dreams and fantasies. In order to bring him back to reality and to the fulfilment of his necessary tasks, psychoanalysis proceeds along the same "false" track of regression which was taken by the libido of the patient, so that at the beginning the analysis looks as if it were supporting his morbid proclivities. But psychoanalysis follows the false tracks of fantasy in order to restore the libido, the valuable part of the fantasies, to consciousness and apply it to the duties of the present. This can only be done by bringing up the unconscious fantasies, together with the libido attached to them. Were there no libido attached, we could safely leave these unconscious fantasies to their own shadowy existence. Unavoidably the patient, feeling confirmed in his regressive tendency by the mere fact of having started the analysis, will, amid increasing resistances, lead the analyst's interest down to the depths of his unconscious shadow-world.

421   It will readily be understood that every analyst, as a normal person, will feel in himself the greatest resistances to the regressive tendency of the patient, as he is quite convinced that this tendency is pathological. As a doctor, he believes he is acting quite rightly not to enter into his patient's fantasies. He is understandably repelled by this tendency, for it is indeed repulsive to see somebody completely given up to such fantasies, finding only himself important and admiring himself unceasingly. Moreover, for the aesthetic sensibilities of the normal person, the average run of neurotic fantasies is exceedingly disagreeable, if not downright disgusting. The psychoanalyst, of course, must put aside all aesthetic value-judgments, just like every other doctor who really wants to help his patient. He must not shudder at dirty work. Naturally there are a great many patients who are physically ill and who do recover through

the application of ordinary physical methods, dietetic or suggestive, without closer exploration and radical treatment. But severe cases can be helped only by a therapy based on an exact investigation and thorough knowledge of the illness. Our psychotherapeutic methods hitherto were general measures of this kind; in mild cases they do no harm, on the contrary they are often of real use. But a great many patients prove inaccessible to these methods. If anything helps here, it is psychoanalysis, which is not to say that psychoanalysis is a cure-all. This is a sneer that comes only from ill-natured criticism. We know very well that psychoanalysis fails in certain cases. As everybody knows, we shall never be able to cure all illnesses.

422   The "diving" work of analysis brings up dirty material, piece by piece, out of the slime, but it must first be cleaned before we can recognize its value. The dirty fantasies are valueless and are thrown aside, but the libido attached to them is of value and this, after the work of cleaning, becomes serviceable again. To the professional psychoanalyst, as to every specialist, it will sometimes seem that the fantasies have a value of their own, and not just the libido. But their value is no concern of the patient's. For the analyst these fantasies have only a scientific value, just as it may be of special interest to the surgeon to know whether the pus contains staphylococci or streptococci. To the patient it is all the same, and so far as he is concerned it is better for the analyst to conceal his scientific interest, lest the patient be tempted to take more pleasure than necessary in his fantasies. The aetiological significance which is attributed to these fantasies—incorrectly, to my mind—explains why so much space is given up to the extensive discussion of all forms of fantasy in the psychoanalytic literature. Once one knows that in this sphere absolutely nothing is impossible, the initial estimation of fantasies will gradually wear itself out, and with it the attempt to discover in them an aetiological significance. Nor will the most exhaustive discussion of case histories ever succeed in emptying this ocean. Theoretically the fantasies in each case are inexhaustible.

423   In most cases, however, the production of fantasies ceases after a time, from which one must not conclude that the possibilities of fantasy are exhausted; the cessation only means that no more libido is regressing. The end of the regressive move-

ment is reached when the libido seizes hold of the actualities of life and is used for the solution of necessary tasks. There are cases, and not a few of them, where the patient continues to produce endless fantasies, whether for his own pleasure or because of the mistaken expectations of the analyst. Such a mistake is especially easy for beginners, since, blinded by psychoanalytic case histories, they keep their interest fixed on the alleged aetiological significance of the fantasies, and are constantly endeavouring to fish up more fantasies from the infantile past, vainly hoping to find there the solution of the neurotic difficulties. They do not see that the solution lies in action, in the fulfilment of certain necessary obligations to life. It will be objected that the neurosis is entirely due to the incapacity of the patient to carry out these tasks, and that, by analysing the unconscious, the therapist ought to enable him to do so, or at least give him the means of doing so.

424   Put in this way, the objection is perfectly true, but we have to add that it is valid only when the patient is really conscious of the task he has to fulfil—conscious of it not only academically, in general theoretical outline, but also in detail. It is characteristic of neurotics to be wanting in this knowledge, although, because of their intelligence, they are well aware of the general duties of life, and struggle perhaps only too hard to fulfil the precepts of current morality. But for that very reason they know all the less, sometimes nothing at all, about the incomparably more important duties to themselves. It is not enough, therefore, to follow the patient blindfold on the path of regression, and to push him back into his infantile fantasies by an untimely aetiological interest. I often hear from patients who have got stuck in a psychoanalytic treatment: "My analyst thinks I must have an infantile trauma somewhere, or a fantasy I am still repressing." Apart from cases where this conjecture happened to be true, I have seen others in which the stoppage was caused by the fact that the libido, hauled up by the analysis, sank back again into the depths for want of employment. This was due to the analyst directing his attention entirely to the infantile fantasies and his failure to see what task of adaptation the patient had to fulfil. The consequence was that the libido always sank back again, as it was given no opportunity for further activity.

425   There are many patients who, quite on their own account, discover their life-tasks and stop the production of regressive fantasies fairly soon, because they prefer to live in reality rather than in fantasy. It is a pity that this cannot be said of all patients. A good many of them postpone the fulfilment of their life-tasks indefinitely, perhaps for ever, and prefer their idle neurotic dreaming. I must emphasize yet again that by "dreaming" we do not mean a conscious phenomenon.

426   In consequence of these facts and insights, the character of psychoanalysis has changed in the course of the years. If in its first stage psychoanalysis was a kind of surgery, which removed the foreign body, the blocked affect, from the psyche, in its later form it was a kind of historical method, which tried to investigate the genesis of the neurosis in all its details and to trace it back to its earliest beginnings.

THE TRANSFERENCE

427   There is no doubt that this method owed its existence not only to a strong scientific interest but also to the personal "empathy" of the analyst, traces of which can clearly be seen in the psychoanalytic case material. Thanks to this personal feeling, Freud was able to discover wherein lay the therapeutic effect of psychoanalysis. While this was formerly sought in the discharge of the traumatic affect, it was now found that the fantasies brought out by analysis were all associated with the person of the analyst. Freud called this process the *transference*, because the patient transferred to the analyst the fantasies that were formerly attached to the memory-images of the parents. The transference is not limited to the purely intellectual sphere; rather, the libido that is invested in the fantasies precipitates itself, together with the fantasies, upon the analyst. All those sexual fantasies which cluster round the imago of the parents now cluster round him, and the less the patient realizes this, the stronger will be his unconscious tie to the analyst.

428   This discovery is of fundamental importance in several ways. Above all, the transference is of great biological value to the patient. The less libido he gives to reality, the more exaggerated will be his fantasies and the more he will be cut off from the

world. Typical of neurotics is their disturbed relationship to reality—that is to say, their reduced adaptation. The transference to the analyst builds a bridge across which the patient can get away from his family into reality. He can now emerge from his infantile milieu into the world of adults, since the analyst represents for him a part of the world outside the family.

429   On the other hand, the transference is a powerful hindrance to the progress of the treatment, because the patient assimilates the analyst, who should stand for a part of the extrafamilial world, to his father and mother, so that the whole advantage of his new acquisition is jeopardized. The more he is able to see the analyst objectively, to regard him as he does any other individual, the greater becomes the advantage of the transference. The less he is able to see the analyst in this way, and the more he assimilates him to the father imago, the less advantageous the transference will be and the greater the harm it will do. The patient has merely widened the scope of his family by the addition of a quasi-parental personality. He himself is, as before, still in the infantile milieu and therefore maintains his infantile constellation. In this manner all the advantages of the transference can be lost.

430   There are patients who follow the analysis with the greatest interest without making the slightest improvement, remaining extraordinarily productive in their fantasies although the whole previous history of their neurosis, even its darkest corners, seems to have been brought to light. An analyst under the influence of the historical view might easily be thrown into confusion, and would have to ask himself: What is there in this case still to be analysed? These are just the cases I had in mind before, when I said it is no longer a matter of analysing the historical material, but of action, of overcoming the infantile attitude. The historical analysis would show over and over again that the patient has an infantile attitude to the analyst, but it would not tell us how to alter it. Up to a certain point, this serious disadvantage of the transference applies to every case. It has gradually proved, even, that the part of psychoanalysis so far discussed, extraordinarily interesting and valuable though it may be from a scientific point of view, is in practice far less important than what now has to follow, namely, the analysis of the transference itself.

CONFESSION AND PSYCHOANALYSIS

431   Before I discuss in detail this especially important part of
the analysis, I should like to draw attention to a parallel between the first stage of psychoanalysis and a certain cultural
institution. By this I mean the religious institution of confession.

432   Nothing makes people more lonely, and more cut off from
the fellowship of others, than the possession of an anxiously
hidden and jealously guarded personal secret. Very often it is
"sinful" thoughts and deeds that keep them apart and estrange
them from one another. Here confession sometimes has a truly
redeeming effect. The tremendous feeling of relief which usually follows a confession can be ascribed to the readmission of
the lost sheep into the human community. His moral isolation
and seclusion, which were so difficult to bear, cease. Herein lies
the chief psychological value of confession.

433   Besides that, however, it has other consequences: through
the transference of his secret and all the unconscious fantasies
underlying it, a moral bond is formed between the patient and
his father confessor. We call this a "transference relationship."
Anyone with psychoanalytic experience knows how much the
personal significance of the analyst is enhanced when the patient
is able to confess his secrets to him. The change this induces in
the patient's behaviour is often amazing. This, too, is an effect
probably intended by the Church. The fact that by far the
greater part of humanity not only needs guidance, but wishes
for nothing better than to be guided and held in tutelage, justi-
fies, in a sense, the moral value which the Church sets on confession. The priest, equipped with all the insignia of paternal
authority, becomes the responsible leader and shepherd of his
flock. He is the father confessor and the members of his parish
are his penitent children.

434   Thus priest and Church replace the parents, and to that extent they free the individual from the bonds of the family. In
so far as the priest is a morally elevated personality with a natural nobility of soul and a mental culture to match, the institution of confession may be commended as a brilliant method of
social guidance and education, which did in fact perform a tre-

mendous educative task for more than fifteen hundred years. So long as the medieval Church knew how to be the guardian of art and science—a role in which her success was due, in part, to her wide tolerance of worldly interests—confession was an admirable instrument of education. But it lost its educative value, at least for more highly developed people, as soon as the Church proved incapable of maintaining her leadership in the intellectual sphere—the inevitable consequence of spiritual rigidity. The more highly developed men of our time do not want to be guided by a creed or a dogma; they want to understand. So it is not surprising if they throw aside everything they do not understand; and religious symbols, being the least intelligible of all, are generally the first to go overboard. The sacrifice of the intellect demanded by a positive belief is a violation against which the conscience of the more highly developed individual rebels.

435   So far as analysis is concerned, in perhaps the majority of cases the transference to and dependence on the analyst could be regarded as a sufficient end with a definite therapeutic effect, provided that the analyst was a commanding personality and in every way capable of guiding his patients responsibly and being a "father to his people." But a modern, mentally developed person strives, consciously or unconsciously, to govern himself and stand morally on his own feet. He wants to take the helm in his own hands; the steering has too long been done by others. He wants to understand; in other words, he wants to be an adult. It is much easier to be guided, but this no longer suits intelligent people today, for they feel that the spirit of the age requires them to exercise moral autonomy. Psychoanalysis has to reckon with this requirement, and has therefore to reject the demand of the patient for constant guidance and instruction. The analyst knows his own shortcomings too well to believe that he could play the role of father and guide. His highest ambition must consist only in educating his patients to become independent personalities, and in freeing them from their unconscious bondage to infantile limitations. He must therefore analyse the transference, a task left untouched by the priest. Through the analysis the unconscious—and sometimes conscious—tie to the analyst is cut, and the patient is set upon his own feet. That, at least, is the aim of the treatment.[2]

2 [Cf. the "Psychology of the Transference" for a more detailed study.]

ANALYSIS OF THE TRANSFERENCE

436   The transference introduces all sorts of difficulties into the relationship between analyst and patient because, as we have seen, the analyst is always more or less assimilated to the family. The first part of the analysis, the discovery of complexes, is fairly easy, thanks to the fact that everyone likes to unburden himself of his painful secrets. Also, he experiences a particular satisfaction in at last finding someone who has an understanding ear for all those things to which nobody would listen before. For the patient it is a singularly agreeable sensation to be understood and to have a doctor who is determined to understand him at all costs, and is willing to follow him, apparently, through all his devious ways. There are patients who even have a special "test" for this, a special question which the analyst has to go into; if he cannot or will not do this, or if he overlooks it, then he is no good. The feeling of being understood is especially sweet to all those lonely souls who are insatiable in their demand for "understanding."

437   For patients with such an obliging disposition, the beginning of the analysis is, as a rule, fairly simple. The therapeutic effects, often considerable, which may appear about this time are easy to obtain, and for that reason they may seduce the beginner into a therapeutic optimism and analytical superficiality which bear no relation to the seriousness and peculiar difficulties of his task. The trumpeting of therapeutic successes is nowhere more contemptible than in psychoanalysis, for no one should know better than the psychoanalyst that the therapeutic result ultimately depends far more on the co-operation of nature and of the patient himself. The psychoanalyst may legitimately pride himself on his increased insight into the essence and structure of neurosis, an insight that greatly exceeds all previous knowledge in this field. But psychoanalytic publications to date cannot be acquitted of the charge of sometimes showing psychoanalysis in a false light. There are technical publications which give the uninitiated person the impression that psychoanalysis is a more or less clever trick, productive of astonishing results.

438   The first stage of the analysis, when we try to understand, and in this way often relieve, the patient's feelings, is responsi-

ble for these therapeutic illusions. The improvements that may appear at the beginning of an analysis are naturally not really results of the treatment, but are generally only passing alleviations which greatly assist the process of transference. After the initial resistances to the transference have been overcome, it turns out to be an ideal situation for a neurotic. He does not need to make any effort himself, and yet someone comes to meet him more than halfway, someone with an unwonted and peculiar wish to understand, who does not allow himself to get bored and is not put off by anything, although the patient sometimes does his utmost to rile him with his wilfulness and childish defiance. This forbearance is enough to melt the strongest resistances, so that the patient no longer hesitates to set the analyst among his family gods, i.e., to assimilate him to the infantile milieu.

439   At the same time, the patient satisfies another need, that is, he achieves a relationship outside the family and thus fulfils a biological demand. Hence the patient obtains a double advantage from the transference relationship: a personality who on the one hand is expected to bestow on him a loving attention in all his concerns, and to that extent is equated with father and mother, but who, on the other hand, is outside the family and thus helps him to fulfil a vitally important and difficult duty without the least danger to himself. When, on top of that, this acquisition is coupled with a marked therapeutic effect, as not infrequently happens, the patient is fortified in his belief that his new-found situation is an excellent one. We can readily appreciate that he is not in the least inclined to give up all these advantages. If it were left to him, he would prefer to remain united with the analyst for ever. Accordingly, he now starts to produce numerous fantasies showing how this goal might be attained. Eroticism plays a large role here, and is exploited and exaggerated in order to demonstrate the impossibility of separation. The patient, understandably enough, puts up the most obstinate resistance when the analyst tries to break the transference relationship.

440   We must not forget, however, that for a neurotic the acquisition of an extrafamilial relationship is one of life's duties, as it is for everyone, and a duty which till then he has either not fulfilled at all or fulfilled in a very limited way. At this point I

must energetically oppose the view one so often hears that an extrafamilial relationship always means a sexual relationship. ⟨In many cases one would like to say: it is precisely not that. It is a favourite neurotic misunderstanding that the right attitude to the world is found by indulgence in sex. In this respect, too, the literature of psychoanalysis is not free from misrepresentations; indeed there are publications from which no other conclusions can be drawn. This misunderstanding is far older than psychoanalysis, however, and so cannot be laid altogether at its door. The experienced medical man knows this advice very well, and I have had more than one patient who has acted according to this prescription. But when a psychoanalyst recommends it, he is making the same mistake as his patient, who believes that his sexual fantasies come from pent-up ("repressed") sexuality. If that were so, this recipe would naturally be a salutary one. It is not a question of that at all, but of regressive libido which exaggerates the fantasies because it evades the real task and strives back to the infantile level.⟩ If we support this regressive tendency at all points we simply reinforce the infantile attitude from which the neurotic is suffering. He has to learn the higher adaptation which life demands from mature and civilized people. Those who have a decided tendency to sink lower will proceed to do so; they need no psychoanalysis for that.

441   At the same time, we must be careful that we do not fall into the opposite extreme of thinking that psychoanalysis creates nothing but quite exceptional personalities. Psychoanalysis stands outside traditional morality; for the present it should adhere to no general moral standard. It is, and should be, only a means for giving the individual trends breathing-space, for developing them and bringing them into harmony with the rest of the personality. It should be a biological method, whose aim is to combine the highest subjective well-being with the most valuable biological performance. As man is not only an individual but also a member of society, these two tendencies inherent in human nature can never be separated, or the one subordinated to the other, without doing him serious injury.

442   The best result for a person who undergoes an analysis is that he shall become in the end what he really is, in harmony with himself, neither good nor bad, just as he is in his natural state. Psychoanalysis cannot be considered a method of educa-

tion, if by education we mean the topiary art of clipping a tree into a beautiful artificial shape. But those who have a higher conception of education will prize most the method of cultivating a tree so that it fulfils to perfection its own natural conditions of growth. We yield too much to the ridiculous fear that we are at bottom quite impossible beings, that if everyone were to appear as he really is a frightful social catastrophe would ensue. Many people today take "man as he really is" to mean merely the eternally discontented, anarchic, rapacious element in human beings, quite forgetting that these same human beings have also erected those firmly established forms of civilization which possess greater strength and stability than all the anarchic undercurrents. ⟨The strengthening of his social personality is one of the essential conditions for man's existence. Were it not so, humanity would cease to be. The selfishness and rebelliousness we meet in the neurotic's psychology are not "man as he really is" but an infantile distortion. In reality the normal man is "civic-minded and moral"; he created his laws and observes them, not because they are imposed on him from without—that is a childish delusion—but because he loves law and order more than he loves disorder and lawlessness.⟩

RESOLUTION OF THE TRANSFERENCE

443   In order to resolve the transference, we have to fight against forces which are not merely neurotic but have a general significance for normal human beings. In trying to get the patient to break the transference relationship, we are asking of him something that is seldom, or never, demanded of the average person, namely, that he should conquer himself completely. Only certain religions demanded this of the individual, and it is this that makes the second stage of analysis so very difficult.

444   ⟨As you know, it is an habitual prejudice of children to think that love gives them the right to make demands. The infantile conception of loving is getting presents from others. Patients make demands in accordance with this definition, and thus behave no differently from most normal people, whose infantile cupidity is only prevented from reaching too high a pitch by their fulfilling their duties to life and by the satisfaction this

affords the libido, and also because a certain lack of tempera-
ment does not incline them from the start to passionate behaviour. The basic trouble with the neurotic is that, instead of
adapting himself to life in his own special way, which would
require a high degree of self-discipline, he makes infantile demands and then begins to bargain. The analyst will hardly be
disposed to comply with the demands the patient makes on him
personally, but circumstances may arise in which he will seek to
buy his freedom with compromises. For instance, he might
throw out hints of moral liberties which, if turned into a maxim,
would bring about a general lowering of the cultural level. But
in that way the patient merely sinks to the lower level and becomes inferior. Nor is it, in the end, a question of culture at all,
but simply of the analyst buying his way out of the constricting
transference situation by offering other, alleged advantages. It
goes against the real interests of the patient to hold out these
compensating advantages so enticingly; at that rate he will never
be freed from his infantile cupidity and indolence. Only self-
conquest can free him from these.

445   The neurotic has to prove that he, just as much as a normal
person, can live reasonably. Indeed, he must do more than a
normal person, he must give up a large slice of his infantilism,
which nobody asks a normal person to do.

446   Patients often try to convince themselves, by seeking out
special adventures, that it is possible to go on living in an infantile way. It would be a great mistake if the analyst tried to
stop them. There are experiences which one must go through
and for which reason is no substitute. Such experiences are often
of inestimable value to the patient.

447   Nowhere more clearly than at this stage of the analysis will
everything depend on how far the analyst has been analysed
himself. If he himself has an infantile type of desire of which he
is still unconscious, he will never be able to open his patient's
eyes to this danger. It is an open secret that all through the analysis intelligent patients are looking beyond it into the soul of
the analyst, in order to find there the confirmation of the healing formulae—or its opposite. It is quite impossible, even by
the subtlest analysis, to prevent the patient from taking over
instinctively the way in which his analyst deals with the problems of life. Nothing can stop this, for personality teaches more

than thick tomes full of wisdom. All the disguises in which he wraps himself in order to conceal his own personality avail him nothing; sooner or later he will come across a patient who calls his bluff. An analyst who from the first takes his profession seriously is faced with the inexorable necessity of testing out the principles of psychoanalysis on himself as well. He will be astonished to see how many apparently technical difficulties vanish in this way. Note that I am not speaking of the initial stage of analysis, which might be called the stage of unearthing the complexes, but of this final, extraordinarily tricky stage which is concerned with the resolution of the transference.

448   I have frequently found that beginners look upon the transference as an entirely abnormal phenomenon that has to be "fought against." Nothing could be more mistaken. To begin with we have to regard the transference merely as a falsification, a sexualized caricature, of the social bond which holds human society together and which also produces close ties between people of like mind. This bond is one of the most valuable social factors imaginable, and it would be a cruel mistake to reject absolutely these social overtures on the part of the patient. It is only necessary to purge them of their regressive components, their infantile sexualism. If that is done, the transference becomes a most convenient instrument of adaptation.

449   The only danger—and it is a great one—is that the unacknowledged infantile demands of the analyst may identify themselves with the parallel demands of the patient. The analyst can avoid this only by submitting to a rigorous analysis at the hands of another. He then learns to understand what analysis really means and how it feels to experience it on your own psyche. Every intelligent analyst will at once see how much this must redound to the benefit of his patients. There are analysts who believe that they can get along with a self-analysis. This is Munchausen psychology, and they will certainly remain stuck. They forget that one of the most important therapeutically effective factors is subjecting yourself to the objective judgment of another. As regards ourselves we remain blind, despite everything and everybody. The analyst, of all people, must give up all isolationist tactics and autoerotic mystification if he wants to help his patients to become socially mature and independent personalities.

450   I know that I am also at one with Freud when I set it up as a
self-evident requirement that a psychoanalyst must discharge
his own duties to life in the proper way. If he does not, nothing
can stop his unutilized libido from automatically descending on
his patients and in the end falsifying the whole analysis. Immature and incompetent persons who are themselves neurotic and
stand with only one foot in reality generally make nothing but
nonsense out of analysis. *Exempla sunt odiosa!* Medicine in the
hand of a fool was ever poison and death. Just as we demand
from a surgeon, besides his technical knowledge, a skilled hand,
courage, presence of mind, and power of decision, so we must
expect from an analyst a very serious and thorough psychoanalytic training of his own personality before we are willing to
entrust a patient to him. I would even go so far as to say that
the acquisition and practice of the psychoanalytic technique
presuppose not only a specific psychological gift but in the very
first place a serious concern with the moulding of one's own
character.)

451   The technique for resolving the transference is the same as
the one we have already described. The problem of what the
patient is to do with the libido he has withdrawn from the person of the analyst naturally occupies a large place. Here too the
danger for the beginner is great, as he will be inclined to suggest or to give advice. For the patient the analyst's efforts in this
respect are extremely convenient, and therefore fatal. At this
important juncture, as everywhere in psychoanalysis, we have
to let the patient and his impulses take the lead, even if the path
seems a wrong one. Error is just as important a condition of
life's progress as truth.

THE PROSPECTIVE FUNCTION OF DREAMS

452   In this second stage of analysis, with its hidden reefs and
shoals, we owe an enormous amount to dreams. At the beginning of the analysis, dreams helped us chiefly to discover the
fantasies; but here they are often extremely valuable guides to
the use of libido. Freud's work laid the foundation for an im-
mense increase in our knowledge in regard to the determination
of the manifest dream content by historical material and wish-

ful tendencies. He showed how dreams give access to a mass of subliminal material, mostly memories that have sunk below the threshold. In keeping with his genius for the purely historical method, Freud's procedure is predominantly analytical. Although this method is incontestably of great value we ought not to adopt this standpoint exclusively, as a one-sided historical view does not take sufficient account of the teleological significance of dreams (stressed in particular by Maeder [3]). Unconscious thinking would be quite inadequately characterized if we considered it only from the standpoint of its historical determinants. For a complete evaluation we have unquestionably to consider its teleological or prospective significance as well. If we pursued the history of the English Parliament back to its earliest beginnings, we should undoubtedly arrive at an excellent understanding of its development and the way its present form was determined. But that would tell us nothing about its prospective function, that is, about the tasks it has to accomplish now and in the future.

453   The same is true of dreams, whose prospective function alone was valued in the superstitions of all times and races. There may well be a good deal of truth in this view. Without presuming to say that dreams have prophetic foresight, it is nevertheless possible that we might find, in this subliminal material, combinations of future events which are subliminal simply because they have not yet attained the degree of clarity necessary for them to become conscious. Here I am thinking of those dim presentiments we sometimes have of the future, which are nothing but very faint, subliminal combinations of events whose objective value we are not yet able to apperceive.

454   The future tendencies of the patient are elaborated with the help of these teleological components of the dream. If this work is successful, the patient passes out of the treatment and out of the semi-infantile transference relationship into a life which has been carefully prepared within him, which he has chosen himself, and to which, after mature deliberation, he can declare himself committed.

[3] ["Die Symbolik in den Legenden, Märchen, Gebräuchen und Träumen" (1908). —EDITORS.]

ability to enter into someone else's experience

FUTURE USES OF PSYCHOANALYSIS

455   As will readily be understood, psychoanalysis can never be
used for polyclinical work. It must always remain in the hands
of the few who, because of their innate educative and psychological capacities, have a particular aptitude and a special
liking for this profession. Just as not every doctor makes a good
surgeon, not everyone is fitted to be a psychoanalyst. The predominantly psychological nature of the work will make it difficult for the medical profession to monopolize it. Sooner or later
other branches of science will master the method, either for
practical reasons or out of theoretical interest. So long as ortho-
dox science excludes psychoanalysis from general discussion as
sheer nonsense, we cannot be surprised if other departments
learn to master the material before the medical profession does.
This is all the more likely as psychoanalysis is a general method
of psychological research and a heuristic principle of the first
rank in the domain of the humane sciences.

456   It is chiefly the work of the Zurich school that has demonstrated the applicability of psychoanalysis as a method of investigation in mental disease. Psychoanalytic investigation of
dementia praecox, for instance, has given us most valuable insights into the psychological structure of this remarkable disease.
It would lead me too far afield to go at all deeply into the results
of these investigations. The theory of the psychological determinants of this disease is a sufficiently vast territory in itself, and
if I were to discuss the symbolistic problems of dementia praecox I would have to put before you a mass of material which
I could not hope to deploy within the framework of these lectures, whose purpose is to provide a general survey.

457   The question of dementia praecox has become so extraordinarily complicated because the recent incursion of psychoanalysis into the domains of mythology and comparative religion
has afforded us deep insight into ethnological symbolism. Those
who were familiar with the symbolism of dreams and of dementia praecox were astounded by the parallelism between the
symbols found in modern individuals and those found in the
history of the human race. Most startling of all is the parallelism
between ethnic and schizophrenic symbols. The complicated

relations between psychology and mythology make it impossible for me to discuss in detail my views on dementia praecox. For the same reason I must refrain from discussing the results of the psychoanalytic investigation of mythology and comparative religion. The principal result of these investigations at present is the discovery of far-reaching parallels between ethnic and individual symbolisms. We cannot yet see what vast perspectives this ethnopsychology may open out. But, from all we know at present, we may expect that psychoanalytic research into the nature of subliminal processes will be enormously enriched and deepened by a study of mythology.

9. A CASE OF NEUROSIS IN A CHILD

458   In these lectures I have had to confine myself to giving you a general account of the nature of psychoanalysis. Detailed discussion of the method and theory would have required a mass of case material, exposition of which would have detracted from a comprehensive view of the whole. But, in order to give you some idea of the actual process of psychoanalytic treatment, I have decided to present a fairly short analysis of an eleven-year-old girl. The case was analysed by my assistant, Miss Mary Moltzer. I must preface my remarks by saying that this case is no more typical of the length or course of an ordinary psychoanalysis than one individual is typical of all others. Nowhere is the abstraction of generally valid rules so difficult as in psychoanalysis, for which reason it is better not to make too many formulations. We must not forget that, notwithstanding the great uniformity of conflicts and complexes, every case is unique, because every individual is unique. Every case demands the analyst's individual interest, and in every case the course of analysis is different.

459   In presenting this case, therefore, I am offering but a small section of the infinitely varied world of the psyche, showing all those apparently bizarre and arbitrary peculiarities which the whim of so-called chance scatters into a human life. It is not my intention to withhold any of the more interesting psychoanalytic details, as I do not want to evoke the impression that psychoanalysis is a rigidly formalistic method. The scientific needs of the investigator prompt him always to look for rules and categories in which the most alive of all living things can be captured. The analyst and observer, on the other hand, must eschew formulas and let the living reality work upon him in all its lawless profusion. Thus I shall try to present this case in its natural setting, and I hope I shall succeed in showing you how differently an analysis develops from what might have been expected on purely theoretical grounds.

460   The case in question is that of an intelligent eleven-year-old girl of good family.

461   The clinical history is as follows: She had to leave school several times on account of sudden nausea and headaches, and was obliged to go to bed. In the morning she sometimes refused to get up and go to school. She suffered from bad dreams, was moody and unreliable. I informed the mother, who came to consult me, that these might be the signs of a neurosis, and that something special might be hidden behind them about which one would have to ask the child. This conjecture was not an arbitrary one, for every attentive observer knows that if children are so restless and bad-tempered something is worrying them.

462   The child now confessed to her mother the following story. She had a favourite teacher, on whom she had a crush. During this last term she had fallen behind with her work, and she thought she had sunk in her teacher's estimation. She then began to feel sick during his lessons. She felt not only estranged from her teacher, but even rather hostile to him. She directed all her friendly feelings to a poor boy with whom she usually shared the bread she took to school. She now gave him money as well, so that he could buy bread for himself. Once, in conversation with this boy, she made fun of her teacher and called him a goat. The boy attached himself to her more and more, and considered that he had the right to levy an occasional tribute from her in the form of a little present of money. Then she became afraid that the boy would tell the teacher she had called him a goat, and she promised him two francs if he would give her his solemn word never to say anything to the teacher. From that moment the boy began to blackmail her; he demanded money with threats, and persecuted her with his demands on the way to school. She was in despair. Her attacks of sickness were closely connected with this story; yet, after the affair had been settled as a result of this confession, her peace of mind was not restored as we would have expected.

463   Very often, as I mentioned in the previous lecture, the mere relation of a painful episode has a favourable therapeutic effect.

Generally this does not last very long, although on occasion it may be maintained for a long time. Such a confession is naturally a long way from being an analysis, despite the fact that there are many nerve specialists nowadays who believe that an analysis is only a somewhat more extensive anamnesis or confession.

464   Not long afterwards, the child had a violent attack of coughing and missed school for one day. After that she went back to school for one day and felt perfectly well. On the third day a renewed attack of coughing came on, with pains on the left side, fever and vomiting. She had a temperature of 103° F. The doctor feared pneumonia. But the next day everything had disappeared again. She felt quite well, and there was no trace of fever or nausea.

465   But still our little patient wept the whole time and did not wish to get up. From this strange course of events I suspected a serious neurosis, and I therefore advised analytical treatment.

FIRST INTERVIEW

466   The little girl seemed nervous and constrained, now and then giving a disagreeable forced laugh. She was first of all given an opportunity to talk about what it felt like to be allowed to stay in bed. We learn that it was especially nice then, as she always had company. Everybody came to see her; best of all, she could get herself read to by Mama, from a book with the story in it of a *prince who was ill and only got well again when his wish was fulfilled, the wish being that his little friend, a poor boy, might be allowed to stay with him.*

467   The obvious relation between this story and her own little love-story, as well as its connection with her sickness, was pointed out to her, whereupon she began to weep, saying that she would rather go with the other children and play with them, or they would run away. This was at once allowed, and away she ran, but came back again in no time, somewhat crestfallen. It was explained to her that she had not run away because she was afraid her playmates would run away, but that she herself wanted to run away because of resistances.

468   At the second interview she was less anxious and inhibited. The conversation was led round to the teacher, but she was too embarrassed to speak about him. Finally came the shamefaced admission that she liked him very much. It was explained to her that she need not be ashamed of that; on the contrary, her love was a guarantee that she would do her very best in his lessons. "So then I may like him?" asked the little patient with a happier face.

469   This explanation justified the child in her choice of a love-object. She had, it seemed, been afraid to admit to herself her feelings for the teacher. It is not easy to explain why this should be so. It was previously assumed that the libido has great difficulty in seizing upon a person outside the family because it still finds itself caught in the incestuous bond—a very plausible view indeed, from which it is difficult to withdraw. On the other hand, it must be emphasized that her libido had taken vehement possession of the poor boy, and he too was someone outside the family, so that the difficulty cannot lie in transferring libido to an extra-familial object, but in some other circumstance. Her love for the teacher was for her a more difficult task, it demanded much more from her than her love for the boy, which did not require any moral effort on her part. The hint dropped in the analysis that love would enable her to do her best brought the child back to her real task, which was to adapt to the teacher.

470   Now if the libido draws back from a necessary task, it does so for the very human reason of indolence, which is particularly marked not only in children but also in primitives and animals. Primitive inertia and laziness are the primary reason for not making the effort to adapt. The libido which is not used for this purpose stagnates, and will then make the inevitable regression to former objects or modes of adaptation. The result is a striking activation of the incest complex. The libido withdraws from the object which is so difficult to attain and which demands such great efforts, and turns instead to the easier ones, and finally to the easiest of all, the infantile fantasies, which are then elaborated into real incest fantasies. The fact that, whenever there is a disturbance of psychological adaptation, we always find an

125

excessive development of these fantasies must likewise be conceived, as I pointed out before, as a regressive phenomenon. That is to say, the incest fantasy is of secondary and not of causal significance, while the primary cause is the resistance of human nature to any kind of exertion. Accordingly, drawing back from certain tasks cannot be explained by saying that man prefers the incestuous relationship, rather he falls back into it because he shuns exertion. Otherwise we would have to say that resistance to conscious effort is identical with preference for the incestuous relationship. This would be obvious nonsense, since not only primitive man but animals too have a mighty dislike of all intentional effort, and are addicted to absolute laziness until circumstances prod them into action. Neither of primitive people nor of animals can it be asserted that preference for incestuous relationships is the cause of their aversion to efforts at adaptation, for, especially in the case of animals, there can be absolutely no question of an incestuous relationship.

471   Characteristically, the child expressed joy not at the prospect of doing her best for the teacher but at being allowed to love him. That was the thing she heard first, because it suited her best. Her relief came from the confirmation that she was justified in loving him—even without making any special effort first.

472   The conversation then went on to the story of the blackmail, which she told again in detail. We learn, furthermore, that she tried to force open her money-box, and when she did not succeed she tried to steal the key from her mother. She also made a clean breast of the other matter: she had made fun of the teacher because he was much nicer to the other girls than to her. But it was true that she had got worse at his lessons, especially in arithmetic. Once she did not understand something, but had not dared to ask for fear of losing the teacher's esteem. Consequently she made mistakes, fell behind, and really did lose it. As a result, she got into a very unsatisfactory position with her teacher.

473   About this time it happened that a girl in her class was sent home because she felt sick. Soon after, the same thing happened to her. In this way, she tried to get away from school, which she no longer liked. The loss of her teacher's esteem led her, on the one hand, to insult him and, on the other, into the affair with the little boy, obviously as a compensation for her lost relation-

ship with the teacher. The explanation she was now given was a simple hint: she would be doing her teacher a good turn if she took pains to understand his lessons by asking questions in time. I may add that this hint had good results; from that moment the little girl became the best pupil and missed no more arithmetic lessons.

474   A point worth stressing in the story of the blackmail is its compulsive character and the lack of freedom it shows in the girl. This is a quite regular phenomenon. As soon as anyone permits his libido to draw back from a necessary task, it becomes autonomous and, regardless of the protests of the subject, chooses its own goals and pursues them obstinately. It is therefore quite common for a person leading a lazy and inactive life to be peculiarly prone to the compulsion of libido, that is, to all kinds of fears and involuntary constraints. The fears and superstitions of primitives furnish the best proof of this, but the history of our own civilization, especially the civilization of antiquity, provides ample confirmation as well. Non-employment of the libido makes it ungovernable. But we must not believe that we can save ourselves permanently from the compulsion of libido by forced efforts. Only to a very limited extent can we consciously set tasks for the libido; other natural tasks are chosen by the libido itself because it is destined for them. If these tasks are avoided, even the most industrious life avails nothing, for we have to consider all the conditions of human nature. Innumerable neurasthenias from overwork can be traced back to this cause, for work done amid internal conflicts creates nervous exhaustion.

THIRD INTERVIEW

475   The girl related a dream she had had when she was five years old, which made an unforgettable impression on her. "I'll never forget the dream as long as I live," she said. I would like to add here that such dreams are of quite special interest. The longer a dream remains spontaneously in the memory, the greater is the importance to be attributed to it. This is the dream: *"I was in a wood with my little brother, looking for strawberries. Then a wolf came and jumped at me. I fled up a staircase, the wolf*

after me. I fell down and the wolf bit me in the leg. I awoke in deadly fear."

476   Before we take up the associations given us by the little girl, I will try to form an arbitrary opinion as to the possible content of the dream, and then see how our results compare with the associations given by the child. The beginning of the dream reminds us of the well-known fairytale of Little Red Ridinghood, which is, of course, known to every child. The wolf ate the grandmother first, then took her shape, and afterwards ate Little Red Ridinghood. But the hunter killed the wolf, cut open the belly, and Little Red Ridinghood sprang out safe and sound.

477   This motif is found in countless myths all over the world, and is the motif of the Bible story of Jonah. The meaning immediately lying behind it is astro-mythological: the sun is swallowed by the sea monster and is born again in the morning. Of course, the whole of astro-mythology is at bottom nothing but psychology—unconscious psychology—projected into the heavens; for myths never were and never are made consciously, they arise from man's unconscious. This is the reason for the sometimes miraculous similarity or identity of myth-forms among races that have been separated from each other in space ever since time began. It explains, for instance, the extraordinary distribution of the cross symbol, quite independently of Christianity, of which America offers specially remarkable examples. It is not possible to suppose that myths were created merely in order to explain meteorological or astronomical processes; they are, in the first instance, manifestations of unconscious impulses, comparable to dreams. These impulses were actuated by the regressive libido in the unconscious. The material which comes to light is naturally infantile material—fantasies connected with the incest complex. Thus, in all these so-called solar myths, we can easily recognize infantile theories about procreation, birth, and incestuous relations. In the fairytale of Little Red Ridinghood it is the fantasy that the mother has to eat something which is like a child, and that the child is born by cutting open the mother's body. This fantasy is one of the commonest and can be found everywhere.

478   From these general psychological considerations we can conclude that the child, in this dream, was elaborating the problem

of procreation and birth. As to the wolf, we must probably put him in the father's place, for the child unconsciously attributed to the father any act of violence towards the mother. This motif, too, is based on countless myths dealing with the violation of the mother. With regard to the mythological parallels, I would like to call your attention to the work of Boas,[1] which includes a magnificent collection of American Indian sagas; then the book by Frobenius, *Das Zeitalter des Sonnengottes;* and finally the works of Abraham, Rank, Riklin, Jones, Freud, Maeder, Silberer, and Spielrein,[2] and my own investigations in *Symbols of Transformation.*

479   After these general reflections, which I give here for theoretical reasons but which naturally formed no part of the treatment, we will go on to see what the child has to tell us about her dream. Needless to say, she was allowed to speak about her dream just as she liked, without being influenced in any way. She picked first on the bite in the leg, and explained that *she had once been told by a woman who had had a baby that she could still show the place where the stork had bitten her.* This expression is, in Switzerland, a variant of the widespread symbolism of copulation and birth. Here we have a perfect parallelism between our interpretation and the association process of the child. For the first association she produced, quite uninfluenced, goes back to the problem we conjectured above on theoretical grounds. I know that the innumerable cases published in the psychoanalytic literature, which were definitely not influenced, have not been able to quash our critics' contention that we suggest our interpretations to the patients. This case, too, will convince no one who is determined to impute to us the crude mistakes of beginners—or, what is worse, falsification.

480   After this first association the little patient was asked what the wolf made her think of. She answered, "I think of my father when he is angry." This, too, coincides absolutely with our theoretical considerations. It might be objected that these considerations were made expressly for this purpose and therefore lack general validity. I think this objection vanishes of itself as soon as one has the requisite psychoanalytic and mythological

[1] [The anthropologist Franz Boas (1858–1942); see especially his *Indianische Sagen* (1895).—EDITORS.]   [2] [See Bibliography.]

knowledge. The validity of a hypothesis can be seen only on the basis of the right knowledge, otherwise not at all.

481   The first association put the stork in the place of the wolf; the association to the wolf now brings us to the father. In the popular myth the stork stands for the father, for he brings the children. The apparent contradiction between the fairytale, where the wolf is the mother, and the dream, where the wolf is the father, is of no importance for the dream or the dreamer. We can therefore dispense with a detailed explanation. I have dealt with this problem of bisexual symbols in my book.[3] As you know, in the legend of Romulus and Remus both animals, the bird Picus and the wolf, were raised to the rank of parents.

482   Her fear of the wolf in the dream is therefore her fear of the father. The dreamer explained that she was afraid of her father because he was very strict with her. He had also told her that we have bad dreams only when we have done something wrong. She then asked her father, "But what does Mama do wrong? She always has bad dreams."

483   Once her father slapped her because she was sucking her finger. She kept on doing this despite his prohibition. Was this, perhaps, the wrong she had done? Hardly, because sucking the finger was simply a rather anachronistic infantile habit, of little real interest at her age, and serving more to irritate her father so that he would punish her by slapping. In this way she relieved her conscience of an unconfessed and much more serious "sin": *it came out that she had induced a number of girls of her own age to perform mutual masturbation.*

484   It was because of these sexual interests that she was afraid of her father. But we must not forget that she had the wolf dream in her fifth year. At that time these sexual acts had not been committed. Hence we must regard the affair with the other girls at most as a reason for her present fear of her father, but that does not explain her earlier fear. Nevertheless, we may expect that it was something similar, some unconscious sexual wish in keeping with the psychology of the forbidden act just mentioned. The character and moral evaluation of this act are naturally far more unconscious to a child than to an adult. In order to understand what could have made an impression on

8 [Cf. *Symbols of Transformation*, particularly par. 547.]

the child so early, we have to ask what happened in her fifth year. *That was the year in which her younger brother was born.* So even then she was afraid of her father. The associations already discussed show us the unmistakable connection between her sexual interests and her fear.

485   The problem of sex, which nature connects with positive feelings of pleasure, appears in the wolf dream in the form of fear, apparently on account of the bad father, who stands for moral education. The dream was therefore the first impressive manifestation of the sexual problem, obviously stimulated by the recent birth of a younger brother, when as we know all these questions become aired. But because the sexual problem was connected at all points with the history of certain pleasurable physical sensations which education devalues as "bad habits," it could apparently manifest itself only in the guise of moral guilt and fear.

486   This explanation, plausible though it is, seems to me superficial and inadequate. We then attribute the whole difficulty to moral education, on the unproven assumption that education can cause a neurosis. This is to disregard the fact that even people with no trace of moral education become neurotic and suffer from morbid fears. Furthermore, moral law is not just an evil that has to be resisted, but a necessity born from the innermost needs of man. Moral law is nothing other than an outward manifestation of man's innate urge to dominate and control himself. This impulse to domestication and civilization is lost in the dim, unfathomable depths of man's evolutionary history and can never be conceived as the consequence of laws imposed from without. Man himself, obeying his instincts, created his laws. We shall never understand the reasons for the fear and suppression of the sexual problem in a child if we take into account only the moral influences of education. The real reasons lie much deeper, in human nature itself, perhaps in that tragic conflict between nature and culture, or between individual consciousness and collective feeling.

487   Naturally, it would have been pointless to give the child a notion of the higher philosophical aspects of the problem; it would certainly have had not the slightest effect. It was sufficient to remove the idea that she was doing something wrong in being interested in the procreation of life. So it was made clear to her

how much pleasure and curiosity she was bringing to bear on the problem of generation, and how her groundless fear was only pleasure turned into its opposite. The affair of her masturbation met with tolerant understanding, and the discussion was limited to drawing the child's attention to the aimlessness of her action. At the same time, it was explained to her that her sexual actions were mainly an outlet for her curiosity, which she might satisfy in a better way. Her great fear of her father expressed an equally great expectation, which because of the birth of her little brother was closely connected with the problem of generation. These explanations justified the child in her curiosity. With that, a large part of the moral conflict was removed.

FOURTH INTERVIEW

488   The little girl was now much nicer and much more confiding. Her former constrained and unnatural manner had quite disappeared. She brought a dream which she dreamt after the last interview. It ran: *"I am as tall as a church-spire and can see into every house. At my feet are very small children, as small as flowers are. A policeman comes. I say to him, 'If you dare to make any remark, I shall take your sword and cut off your head.'"*

489   In the analysis of the dream she made the following remark: "I would like to be taller than my father, because then he would have to obey me." She at once associated the policeman with her father, who was a military man and had, of course, a sword. The dream clearly fulfils her wish. As a church-spire, she is much bigger than her father, and if he dares to make a remark he will be decapitated. The dream also fulfils the natural wish of the child to be "big," i.e., grown-up, and to have children playing at her feet. In this dream she got over her fear of her father, and from this we may expect a significant increase in her personal freedom and feeling of security.

490   On the theoretical side, we may regard this dream as a clear example of the compensatory significance and teleological function of dreams. Such a dream must leave the dreamer with a heightened sense of the value of her own personality, and this is of great importance for her personal well-being. It does not

matter that the symbolism was not clear to the consciousness of the child, for the emotional effect of symbols does not depend on conscious understanding. It is more a matter of intuitive knowledge, the source from which all religious symbols derive their efficacy. Here no conscious understanding is needed; they influence the psyche of the believer through intuition.

FIFTH AND SIXTH INTERVIEWS

491   The child related the following dream which she had dreamt in the meantime: *"I was standing with my whole family on the roof. The windows of the houses on the other side of the valley shone like fire. The rising sun was reflected in them. Suddenly I saw that the house at the corner of our street was really on fire. The fire came nearer and nearer and took hold of our house. I ran into the street, and my mother threw all sorts of things after me. I held out my apron, and among other things she threw me a doll. I saw that the stones of our house were burning, but the wood remained untouched."*

492   The analysis of this dream presented peculiar difficulties and had to be extended over two sittings. It would lead me too far to describe the whole of the material this dream brought forth; I shall have to limit myself to what is most essential. The salient associations began with the peculiar image of the stones of the house burning but not the wood. It is sometimes worth while, especially with longer dreams, to take the most striking images and analyse them first. This is not the general rule but it may be excused here by the practical need for abbreviation.

493   "It is queer, like in a fairytale," said the little patient about this image. She was shown, with the help of examples, that fairytales always have a meaning. "But not all fairytales," she objected. "For instance, the tale of Sleeping Beauty. What could that mean?" It was explained to her that Sleeping Beauty had to wait for a hundred years in an enchanted sleep until she could be set free. Only the hero whose love overcame all difficulties and who boldly broke through the thorny hedge could rescue her. Thus one often has to wait for a long time before one obtains one's heart's desire.

494   This explanation was suited to the child's understanding,

and on the other hand was perfectly in accord with the history of this fairytale motif. The tale of Sleeping Beauty has obvious connections with an ancient spring and fertility myth, and at the same time contains a problem which has a remarkably close affinity with the psychological situation of a rather precocious little girl of eleven. It belongs to a whole cycle of legends in which a virgin, guarded by a dragon, is rescued by a hero. Without wishing to embark on an interpretation of this myth, I would like to emphasize its astronomical or meteorological components, clearly brought out in the Edda. The earth, in the form of a maiden, is held prisoner by the winter, and is covered with ice and snow. The young spring sun, the fiery hero, melts her out of her frosty prison, where she had long awaited her deliverer.

495   The association given by the little girl was chosen by her simply as an example of a fairytale without a meaning, and not as a direct association to the dream-image of the burning house. About this she only made the remark, "It is queer, like in a fairytale," by which she meant impossible; for to say that stones burn is something completely impossible, nonsensical, and like a fairytale. The explanation she was given showed her that "impossible" and "like a fairytale" are only partly identical, since fairytales do have a great deal of meaning. Although this particular fairytale, from the casual way it was mentioned, seems to have nothing to do with the dream, it deserves special attention because it appeared, as though by chance, while the dream was being analysed. The unconscious came out with just this example, and this cannot be mere chance but is somehow characteristic of the situation at that moment. In analysing dreams we have to look out for these seeming accidents, for in psychology there are no blind accidents, much as we are inclined to assume that these things are pure chance. You can hear this objection as often as you like from our critics, but for a really scientific mind there are only causal relationships and no accidents. From the fact that the little girl chose Sleeping Beauty as an example we must conclude that there was some fundamental reason for this in the psychology of the child. This reason was the comparison or partial identification of herself with Sleeping Beauty; in other words, in the psyche of the child there was a complex which found expression in the Sleeping Beauty motif.

134

The explanation given to the child took account of this inference.

496   Nevertheless, she was not quite satisfied, and still doubted
that fairytales have a meaning. As a further example of an incomprehensible fairytale she cited Snow White, who lay en-
closed in a glass coffin, in the sleep of death. It is not difficult
to see that Snow White belongs to the same cycle of myths as
Sleeping Beauty. It contains even clearer indications of the myth
of the seasons. The myth material chosen by the child points
to an intuitive comparison with the earth, held fast by the winter's cold, awaiting the liberating sun of spring.

497   This second example confirms the first one and the explanation we have given. It would be difficult to maintain that the
second example, accentuating as it does the meaning of the first,
was suggested by the explanation. The fact that the little girl
gave Snow White as another example of a meaningless fairytale
proves that she did not realize the identity of Snow White and
Sleeping Beauty. We may therefore conjecture that Snow White
arose from the same unconscious source as Sleeping Beauty,
namely, from a complex concerned with the expectation of coming events. These events may be compared exactly with the
deliverance of the earth from the prison of winter and its fertilization by the rays of the spring sun. As you know, from
ancient times the fertilizing spring sun was associated with the
symbol of the bull, the animal embodying the mightiest pro-
creative power. Although we cannot yet see the connection between these insights and the dream, we will hold fast to what
we have gained and proceed with our analysis.

498   The next dream-image shows the little girl catching the doll
in her apron. Her first association tells us that her attitude and
the whole situation in the dream reminded her of *a picture she
knew, showing a stork flying over a village, with little girls standing in the street holding out their aprons and shouting to the
stork to bring them a baby.* She added that she herself had long
wanted a baby brother or sister. This material, given spontaneously, is clearly related to the myth-motifs already discussed. It
is evident that the dream was in fact concerned with the same
problem of the awakening reproductive instinct. Of course,
nothing of these connections was mentioned to the child.

499   Then, abruptly, after a pause, came the next association:

"Once, when I was five years old, I lay down in the street and a bicycle passed over my stomach." This highly improbable story proved to be, as might be expected, a fantasy, which had become a paramnesia. Nothing of the kind had ever happened, but on the other hand we learn that at school *the little girls used to lie crosswise over each other's bodies and trample with their legs.*

500   Anyone who has read the analyses of children published by Freud and myself [4] will recognize in this childish game the same basic motif of trampling, which we considered must have a sexual undercurrent. This view, demonstrated by our earlier work, was borne out by the next association of our little patient: "I would much rather have a real baby than a doll."

501   All this highly remarkable material brought out by the stork fantasy suggests the typical beginnings of an infantile sexual theory, and at the same time shows us the point round which the little girl's fantasies were revolving.

502   It may be of interest to know that the motif of treading or trampling can be found in mythology. I have documented this in my book on libido.[5] The use of these infantile fantasies in the dream, the paramnesia about the bicyclist, and the tense expectation expressed in the Sleeping Beauty motif all show that the child's inner interest was dwelling on certain problems that had to be solved. Probably the fact that her libido was attracted by the problem of generation was the reason why her interest flagged at school, so that she fell behind in her work. How very much this problem fascinates girls of twelve and thirteen I was able to show in a special case, published in "A Contribution to the Psychology of Rumour." [6] It is the cause of all that smutty talk among children, and of mutual attempts at enlightenment which naturally turn out to be very nasty and often ruin the child's imagination for good. Even the most careful protection cannot prevent them from one day discovering the great secret, and then probably in the dirtiest way. It would be far better for children to learn the facts of life cleanly and in good time, so that they would not need to be enlightened in ugly ways by their playmates.

4 [Cf. "Psychic Conflicts in a Child," pars. 47ff.]
5 [*Symbols of Transformation*, pars. 370, 480.]
6 [Cf. supra, pars. 95ff.]

503   These and other indications showed that the moment had come for a certain amount of sexual enlightenment. The little girl listened attentively to the talk that followed, and then asked very seriously: "So then I really can't have a child?" This question led to an explanation about sexual maturity.

SEVENTH INTERVIEW

504   The little girl began by remarking that she perfectly understood why it was not yet possible for her to have a child; she had therefore renounced all idea of it. But this time she did not make a good impression. It turned out that she had lied to her teacher. She had been late to school, and told the teacher that she had had to go somewhere with her father and had therefore arrived late. In reality, she had been too lazy to get up in time. She told a lie because she was afraid of losing the teacher's favour by confessing the truth. This sudden moral defeat requires an explanation. According to the principles of psychoanalysis, a sudden and striking weakness can only come about when the analysand does not draw from the analysis the conclusions that are necessary at the moment, but still keeps the door open to other possibilities. This means, in our case, that though the analysis had apparently brought the libido to the surface, so that an improvement of personality could occur, for some reason or other the adaptation was not made, and the libido slipped back along its old regressive path.

EIGHTH INTERVIEW

505   The eighth interview proved that this was indeed the case. Our patient had withheld an important piece of evidence in regard to her ideas of sex, and one which contradicted the analyst's explanation of sexual maturity. *She had not mentioned a rumour current in the school that a girl of eleven had got a baby from a boy of the same age.* This rumour was proved to be groundless; it was a fantasy, fulfilling the secret wishes of girls of this age. Rumours often start in this way, as I have tried to show in my paper on the psychology of rumour. They air the

unconscious fantasies, and in this function they correspond to dreams and myths. This rumour kept another way open: she need not wait, she could have a child already at eleven. The contradiction between the accepted rumour and the analyst's explanation created resistances against the latter, as a result of which it was immediately devalued. All the other information and instruction fell to the ground at the same time, giving rise to momentary doubt and uncertainty. The libido then took to its former path and became regressive. This moment was the moment of the relapse.

NINTH INTERVIEW

506   This interview contributed some important details to the history of her sexual problem. First came a significant dream fragment: "*I was with other children in a clearing in a wood, surrounded by beautiful fir-trees. It began to rain, there was thunder and lightning, and it grew dark. Then I suddenly saw a stork in the air.*"

507   Before we start analysing this dream, I must mention its parallels with certain mythological ideas. To anyone familiar with the works of Adalbert Kuhn and Steinthal, to which Abraham [7] has recently drawn attention, the curious combination of thunderstorm and stork is not at all surprising. Since ancient times the thunderstorm has had the meaning of an earth-fecundating act, it is the cohabitation of Father Heaven and Mother Earth, where the lightning takes over the role of the winged phallus. The stork in flight is just the same thing, a winged phallus, and its psychosexual meaning is known to every child. But the psychosexual meaning of the thunderstorm is not known to everyone, and certainly not to our little patient. In view of the whole psychological constellation previously described, the stork must unquestionably be given a psychosexual interpretation. The fact that the thunderstorm is connected with the stork and, like it, has a psychosexual meaning seems difficult to accept at first. But when we remember that psychoanalytic research has already discovered a vast number of purely mytholog-

7 [See *Symbols of Transformation*, index, s.vv.—EDITORS.]

ical connections in the unconscious psychic products, we may conclude that the psychosexual link between the two images is present also in this case. We know from other experiences that those unconscious strata which once produced mythological formations are still active in modern individuals and are unceasingly productive. Only, the production is limited to dreams and to the symptomatology of the neuroses and psychoses, as the correction by reality is so strong in the modern mind that it prevents them from being projected upon the real world.

508   To return to the analysis of the dream: the associations that led to the heart of this image began with the idea of *rain during a thunderstorm*. Her actual words were: "I think of water—my uncle was drowned in the water—it must be awful to be stuck in the water like that, in the dark—but wouldn't the baby drown in the water, too? Does it drink the water that is in the stomach? Queer, when I was ill Mama sent my water to the doctor. I thought he was going to mix something with it like syrup, which babies grow from, and Mama would have to drink it."

509   We see with unquestionable clearness from this string of associations that the child connected psychosexual ideas specifically relating to fertilization with the rain during the thunderstorm.

510   Here again we see that remarkable parallelism between mythology and the individual fantasies of our own day. This series of associations is so rich in symbolical connections that a whole dissertation could be written about them. The symbolism of drowning was brilliantly interpreted by the child herself as a pregnancy fantasy, an explanation given in the psychoanalytic literature long ago.

TENTH INTERVIEW

511   The tenth interview was taken up with the child's spontaneous description of infantile theories about fertilization and birth, which could now be dismissed as settled. The child had always thought that the urine of the man went into the body of the woman, and that from this the embryo would grow. Hence the child was in the water, i.e., urine, from the beginning. Another version was that the urine was drunk with the

doctor's syrup, the child grew in the head, the head was then split open to help the child grow, and one wore hats to cover this up. She illustrated this by a little drawing, showing a childbirth through the head. This idea is archaic and highly mythological. I need only remind you of the birth of Pallas Athene, who came out of her father's head. The fertilizing significance of urine is also mythological; we find excellent proofs of this in the Rudra songs of the Rig-veda.[8] I should also mention something which the mother corroborated, that once the little girl, long before the analysis, declared that she saw a jack-in-a-box dancing on her younger brother's head—a fantasy which may well be the origin of this birth-theory.

512   The drawing had a remarkable affinity with certain artefacts found among the Bataks of Sumatra. They are called magic wands or ancestor-columns, and consist of a number of figures standing one on top of another. The explanation given by the Bataks themselves of these columns, and generally regarded as nonsense, is in remarkable agreement with the mentality of a child, still caught in the infantile bonds. They assert that these superimposed figures are members of a family who, because they committed incest, were entwined by a snake while being bitten to death by another snake. This explanation runs parallel with the assumptions of our little patient, for her sexual fantasies, too, as we saw from the first dream, revolved round her father. Here, as with the Bataks, the primary condition is the incest relationship.

513   A third version was the theory that the child grew in the intestinal canal. This version had its own symptomatic phenomenology thoroughly in accord with Freudian theory. The girl, acting on her fantasy that children were "sicked up," frequently tried to induce nausea and vomiting. She also performed regular pushing-exercises in the water-closet, in order to push the child out. In this situation it was not surprising that the first and most important symptoms in the manifest neurosis were those of nausea.

514   We have now got so far with our analysis that we can cast a glance back at the case as a whole. We found, behind the neurotic symptoms, complicated emotional processes that were un-

8 [Cf. *Symbols of Transformation*, par. 322f.]

doubtedly connected with these symptoms. If we may venture to draw general conclusions from such limited material, we can reconstruct the course of the neurosis somewhat as follows.

515 At the gradual approach of puberty, the libido of the child produced in her an emotional rather than an objective attitude to reality. She developed a crush on her teacher, and this sentimental indulgence in starry-eyed fantasies obviously played a greater role than the thought of the increased efforts which such a love really demanded. Consequently, her attention fell off, and her work suffered. This upset her former good relationship with the teacher. He became impatient, and the girl, who had been made over-demanding by conditions at home, grew resentful instead of trying to improve her work. As a result, her libido turned away from the teacher as well as from her work and fell into that characteristically compulsive dependence on the poor young boy, who exploited the situation as much as he could. For when an individual consciously or unconsciously lets his libido draw back from a necessary task, the unutilized (so-called "repressed") libido provokes all sorts of accidents, within and without—symptoms of every description which force themselves on him in a disagreeable way. Under these conditions the girl's resistance to going to school seized on the first available opportunity, which soon presented itself in the form of the other girl who was sent home because she felt sick. Our patient duly copied this.

516 Once out of school, the way was open to her fantasies. Owing to the libido regression, the symptom-creating fantasies were aroused in real earnest and acquired an influence which they never had before, for previously they had never played such an important role. But now they took on a highly significant content and seemed themselves to be the real reason why the libido regressed to them. It might be said that the child, with her fantasy-spinning nature, saw her father too much in the teacher, and consequently developed incestuous resistances against him. As I explained earlier, I think it is simpler and more probable to assume that it was temporarily convenient for her to see her teacher as the father. Since she preferred to follow the secret promptings of puberty rather than her obligations to the school and her teacher, she allowed her libido to pick on the little boy, from whom, as we saw in the analysis, she promised herself

certain secret advantages. Even if the analysis had proved she really did have incestuous resistances against her teacher owing to the transference of the father-imago, these resistances would only have been secondarily blown-up fantasies. The prime mover would in any case be laziness or convenience, or, to put it in more scientific language, the principle of least resistance.

517 ⟨I think there are cogent reasons for assuming—I mention this only in passing—that it is not always a perfectly legitimate interest in sexual processes and their unknown nature that accounts for the regression to infantile fantasies. For we find the same regressive fantasies even in adults who have long known all about sex, and here there is no legitimate reason. It is also my impression that young people in analysis often try to keep up their alleged ignorance, despite enlightenment, in order to direct attention there rather than to the task of adaptation. Although there is no doubt in my mind that children do exploit their real or pretended ignorance, it must on the other hand be stressed that young people have a right to be sexually enlightened. As I said before, for many children it would be a distinct advantage if this were decently done at home.

518 Through the analysis it became clear that independently of the progressive development of the child's life a regressive movement had set in, which caused the neurosis, the disunion with herself.⟩ By following this regressive tendency, the analysis discovered a keen sexual curiosity, circling round quite certain definite problems. The libido, caught in this labyrinth of fantasies, was made serviceable again as soon as the child was freed from the burden of mistaken infantile fantasies by being enlightened. This also opened her eyes to her own attitude to reality and gave her an insight into her true potentialities. The result was that she was able to look at her immature, adolescent fantasies in an objective and critical way, and to give up these and all other impossible desires, using her libido instead for a positive purpose, in her work and in obtaining the goodwill of her teacher. The analysis brought her great peace of mind, as well as marked intellectual improvement in school; for the teacher himself confirmed that the little girl soon became the best pupil in his class.

519 ⟨In principle, this analysis is no different from that of an adult. Only the sexual enlightenment would be dropped, but its

place would be taken by something very similar, namely, enlightenment concerning the infantilism of his previous attitude to reality and how to acquire a more reasonable one. Analysis is a refined technique of Socratic maieutics, and it is not afraid to tread the darkest paths of neurotic fantasy.⟩

520   I hope that with the help of this very condensed example I may have succeeded in giving you some insight not only into the actual course of treatment, and into the difficulties of technique, but no less into the beauty of the human psyche and its endless problems. I have deliberately stressed certain parallels with mythology in order to indicate some of the uses to which psychoanalytic insights may be put. At the same time, I would like to point out the implications of this discovery. The marked predominance of mythological elements in the psyche of the child gives us a clear hint of the way the individual mind gradually develops out of the "collective mind" of early childhood, thus giving rise to the old theory of a state of perfect knowledge before and after individual existence.

521   ⟨These mythological references which we find in children are also met with in dementia praecox and in dreams. They offer a broad and fertile field of work for comparative psychological research. The distant goal to which these investigations lead is a phylogeny of the mind, which, like the body, has attained its present form through endless transformations. The rudimentary organs, as it were, which the mind still possesses can be found in full activity in other mental variants and in certain pathological conditions.⟩

522   With these hints I have now reached the present position of our research, and have sketched out at least those insights and working hypotheses which define the nature of my present and future work. ⟨I have endeavoured to propound certain views, which deviate from the hypotheses of Freud, not as contrary assertions but as illustrations of the organic development of the basic ideas Freud has introduced into science. It would not be fitting to disturb the progress of science by adopting the most contradictory standpoint possible and by making use of an entirely different nomenclature—that is the privilege of the very few; but even they find themselves obliged to descend from their lonely eminence after a time and once more take part in the slow progress of average experience by which ideas are

143

evaluated. I hope, also, that my critics will not again accuse me of having contrived my hypotheses out of thin air. I would never have ventured to override the existing ones had not hundreds of experiences shown me that my views fully stand the test in practice. No great hopes should be set on the results of any scientific work; yet if it should find a circle of readers, I hope it will serve to clear up various misunderstandings and remove a number of obstacles which bar the way to a better comprehension of psychoanalysis. Naturally my work is no substitute for lack of psychoanalytic experience. Anyone who wishes to have his say in these matters will have, now as then, to investigate his cases as thoroughly as was done by the psychoanalytic school.)

PRINCETON/BOLLINGEN PAPERBACK EDITIONS

FROM THE COLLECTED WORKS OF C. G. JUNG

Aion (9b)
Alchemical Studies (13)
Archetypes and the Collective Unconscious (9a)
The Development of Personality (17)
Mysterium Coniunctionis (14)
The Practice of Psychotherapy (16)
Psychological Types (6)
Psychology and Alchemy (12)
Spirit in Man, Art, and Literature (15)
Symbols of Transformation (5)
Two Essays on Analytical Psychology (7)

TOPICAL SELECTIONS FROM THE COLLECTED WORKS

Answer to Job
Aspects of the Feminine
Aspects of the Masculine
Dreams
Flying Saucers
Four Archetypes
Jung contra Freud
On the Nature of the Psyche
Psychology and the East
Psychology and the Occult
Psychology and Western Religion
Synchronicity
The Undiscovered Self

ENCOUNTERING JUNG SERIES

Jung on Active Imagination
Jung on Alchemy ·

Jung on Christianity
Jung on Death and Immortality
Jung on Evil
Jung on Mythology

ANTHOLOGIES, LETTERS, AND STUDIES

The Basic Writings of C. G. Jung
C. G. Jung Speaking
The Essential Jung
The Freud/Jung Letters (abridged edition)
The Gnostic Jung
Psyche and Symbol
Psychological Reflections

SEMINARS

Analytical Psychology: Notes of the Seminar Given in 1925
Children's Dreams: Notes from the Seminar Given in 1936–1940
Introduction to Jungian Psychology: Notes of the Seminar on Analytical
Psychology Given in 1925
Nietzsche's *Zarathustra*: Notes of the Seminar Given in 1934–1939
The Psychology of Kundalini Yoga: Notes of the Seminar Given in 1932